HOW TO
SURVIVE
THE END OF THE
WORLD

HOW TO
SURVIVE
THE END OF THE
WORLD

BOB HOSTETLER

LEAFWOOD
PUBLISHERS

How to Survive the End of the World

Copyright 2012 by Bob Hostetler

ISBN 978-0-89112-325-5
LCCN 2012014905

Printed in the United States of America

Published in association with The Steve Laube Agency, 5025 N. Central Ave., #635, Phoenix, AZ 85012.

Library of Congress Cataloging-in-Publication Data
Hostetler, Bob, 1958-
How to survive the end of the world / by Bob Hostetler.
    p. cm.
ISBN 978-0-89112-325-5
1. Bible. N.T. Revelation—Criticism, interpretation, etc. 2. End of the world—Biblical teaching. I. Title.
BS2825.52.H68 2012
    228'.06—dc23   2012014905

Interior text design by Charles Sutherland, E. T. Lowe Publishing
Cover design by Marc Whitaker, MTWdesign

Leafwood Publishers is an imprint of
Abilene Christian University Press
1626 Campus Court
Abilene, Texas 79601
1-877-816-4455
www.leafwoodpublishers.com

12 13 14 15 16 17 / 7 6 5 4 3 2 1

Dedicated to
Miles, Mia, Calleigh, and Ryder

Table of Contents

Acknowledgments

Thank you—again—to my agent and friend, Steve Laube of the Steve Laube Agency, for representing me on this project.

Thank you to Dr. Leonard Allen, Gary Myers, Robyn Burwell, and all the folks at Leafwood Publishers for believing in this book and its message, for their vision and flexibility, and for the inestimable expertise that made the book better at every point in the process.

Thank you to Eugene Peterson, whose *Reversed Thunder: The Revelation of John and the Praying Imagination* led to the study that led to this book. Thank you to John Johnson, my study and brainstorming partner.

Thank you also—as always—to the lovely Robin, my wife. She inspires me, tolerates me, and encourages me in the ministry of writing.

1

Fire and Ice

Come, divine Interpreter,
Bring me eyes Thy book to read
　　　　　—Charles Wesley

Some say the world will end in fire,
Some say in ice.
From what I've tasted of desire
I hold with those who favor fire.
But if it had to perish twice,
I think I know enough of hate
To say that for destruction ice
Is also great
And would suffice.[1]

So said Robert Frost, who wrote those lines roughly a hundred years ago. That whimsical poem contrasts two theories about the end of the world. But there are at least dozens more, perhaps hundreds. Some people believe the famous Long Count calendar of the ancient Mayans calculated the end of the world to occur at the time of the winter solstice on December 21, 2012.

Radio preacher Harold Camping predicted that Jesus would return on May 21, 2011, an event that he said would be followed by five months of fire and brimstone, plagues and disasters. When that didn't happen, he revised his prediction to October 21. When that didn't happen, he apologized . . . and retired.

On the other hand, astrophysicist Donald Brownlee and paleontologist Peter Ward, in their book *The Life and Death of Planet Earth*, predict the end will come in approximately 7.9 billion years. The advantage of their approach is that, whether they turn out to be right or wrong, they probably won't be around to apologize. And if they are, we probably won't be around to hear it.

Hinduism teaches that the god Vishnu will come back in the last cycle of time riding a white horse and carrying a sword that looks like a comet and destroys evil. Many think we will eventually end up destroying the world ourselves, in a nuclear holocaust or a global pandemic. Others expect a zombie apocalypse, robot rebellion, or alien invasion sometime in the future (I happen to think cell phones will play a key role in the apocalypse, but I'm not yet sure exactly how).

But poet T. S. Eliot had a different vision, in his 1925 poem, *The Hollow Men*.

He said,

> This is the way the world ends
> This is the way the world ends
> This is the way the world ends
> Not with a bang but a whimper.[2]

Apocalyptic Fears

Whether it's with a bang or a whimper—or something else—a lot of people are talking about the end of the world these days. And, though most people have plenty of other things to worry about, it can be a haunting proposition. What if the doomsayers are right? What will happen to me? To my loved ones?

Such questions become more urgent as conditions around us—and the twenty-four-hour news cycle that reports and repeats them, ad nauseam—become gloomier. Economic catastrophe looms. Natural disasters strike. Governments totter and topple. Weird weather patterns. Mutating diseases. It can all be quite overwhelming, and it's not hard to believe that a catastrophe of biblical proportions is right around the corner.

A Christian teen posted on an Internet site:

> for a long time i have, moderate to severe anxiety attacks about death and the end of the world, sometimes they are so bad, i am bawling and clinging to my mom, the attacks and images are very strong, and its very hard to fight. i dont want to go on anymore meds i'm on 9 different meds already, and no the meds dont cause the attacks, i'm confused and i just cant handle these attacks anymore, i'm tired of bein scared, PLEASE help me.[3]

A twenty-three-year-old woman said she became so fearful that the world would end that she couldn't bear to look out the windows at night or at the sky during the day. She became unable to sleep in her upstairs bedroom, seeking refuge in the basement instead.[4]

Fears of the apocalypse have recently become so rampant that an official government agency in France alerted the entire country to the risk of mass suicides prompted by end-of-the-world fears.[5] The French government, which lists at least thirty groups that preach the approaching apocalypse, also worried about citizens fleeing to Bugarach, a tiny village in the southern district of Aude that is expected to survive judgment day, according to some.[6]

Some believe such fears will soon become even more widespread. But it doesn't have to be that way, believe it or not. Not that any of us can change whether the world ends or how it ends or when. But the end of the world doesn't have to be the end. In fact, it can actually be the best of all possible beginnings. If you know how to survive it.

That's what this book is about. It will take you on a journey to infinity . . . and beyond. Through it, you will explore an ancient apocalyptic vision in a fresh, invigorating way. Instead of arcane theories and timelines, you will understand this two-thousand-year-old revelation of "the last days" the way it was meant to be seen and received—as a survivor's guide, a message of blessing and hope, and a tool that will thoroughly prepare you for the end . . . *whenever* it comes. Unlike most approaches to what many consider a confusing and frightening book, *How to Survive the End of the World* will bless you. And inform you. And make your daily life better, fuller, and richer.

Each chapter of *How to Survive the End of the World* ends with a suggested prayer for you to pray. These prayers are intended as a way to further apply and internalize the message of each chapter. Please don't skip them. Take your time with them. Focus your mind and heart on praying them sincerely, and God will do amazing things in answer to your prayers.

Prayer

Lord Jesus, I surrender to you my fears and preconceptions as I begin reading this book. Help me to experience The Revelation in a fresh, invigorating way. Help me to receive it as you intended it, as a message of blessing and hope, that will not only prepare me for your glorious appearing but will also equip and encourage me in the days that remain between now and then. Amen.

2

Apocalypse Approaches

All who read, or hear, are blessed,
If Thy plain commands we do;
Of Thy kingdom here possessed,
Thee we shall in glory view
— Charles Wesley

It was an evil time.

Families were struggling all over the region. Recurring famines were making food staples increasingly expensive, and businesses were closing left and right. The rich were unquestionably getting richer, and the poor were getting poorer—and angrier.

Worse still, for the small Christian community in the area, life was becoming more unpredictable by the day. Many shared in the economic hardships. And few families had escaped the regime's cruelty. Even the most distinguished households had suffered sorely: houses and lands confiscated, a mother or sister banished from the country, a father or brother executed without a trial.

And still conditions worsened. The Roman emperors had long claimed divinity and demanded worship from their subjects. But the current emperor Domitian had intensified the demand that the people worship him as "Lord and God." True followers of Jesus, whose allegiance was to Christ alone, recognized the emperor's actions as the harbinger of a holocaust, the cloud of a coming apocalypse.

One of those Christians, exiled to a tiny, rocky island in the Aegean Sea, was the Apostle John, the "beloved disciple" who had walked the length of Galilee and Judea alongside Jesus himself. He had run afoul of the authorities and so was banished from his hometown of Ephesus and sent to live on the island of Patmos. There, in nearly the last years of his long life, he recorded a series of visions that have been preserved for more than twenty centuries in a book called The Revelation.

The Revelation, also sometimes called The Apocalypse, which comes from the Greek word translated "revelation," is the last book in the Bible. It was also the last to be written, most likely at the very end of the first century, roughly sixty-five years or so after the crucifixion, resurrection, and ascension of the Lord Jesus. It is the last word on a dazzling array of subjects, the closing chapters of God's inspired revelation to his people. It is unique in that respect and in other respects.

It is a form of literature that basically no longer exists in our day, called apocalyptic literature. It is nothing like the zombie stories and dystopian fantasies that sell in bookstores today. This literary form flourished from about two hundred years before Jesus' birth to about two hundred years after. Generally speaking, the only other examples of this literary genre most of us are familiar with are the book of Daniel, a few shorter passages in the Old Testament, and Jesus' words in the twenty-fourth chapter of Matthew in the New Testament.

Partly because it is an example of a literary form that is unfamiliar to us and also because that genre itself is extremely figurative, the book of Revelation has captivated and confused readers and scholars for two thousand years and will probably do so until Jesus returns. But perhaps the main reason The Revelation has generated so much confusion is that so many people have tried to explain it—and understand it—without regard for the book's stated purpose, the reason it was written in the first place.

Whenever, Whoever, and Whatever

There may be more theories about the book of Revelation than there are bad jokes in a Muppet movie. But they can be narrowed down to four basic views about how The Revelation should be interpreted:

> 1. *The "Futurist" View.* This view says that, apart from the first few chapters, the book of Revelation depicts events that immediately precede the Second Coming of Jesus Christ. According to this view, most of the book has yet to be fulfilled (or is being fulfilled now), and its primary value is for Christians who will be alive when Jesus returns. This is the view reflected in the bestselling Left Behind novels by Tim Lahaye and Jerry Jenkins. Among those who hold this view, however, are many different ideas of

how the details shake together. Among futurists, there's the pre-tribulation view, mid-trib, pre-wrath, post-trib, the amillenial view, and the partial rapture view. There's Kingdom Now theology and Dominion theology. These are all different—and sometimes conflicting—parts of the futurist view of The Revelation. And that's just a partial and oversimplified list.

2. *The "Historical" View.* Another theory is that The Revelation provides a panoramic view of the church throughout history. This view finds in the book such events as the rise of Islam, the development of Catholicism, the Protestant reformation, world wars, and more, ending with the return of Christ. In this view, The Revelation is intended to encourage readers who recognize the pattern by giving them a historical context for the particular trials and afflictions of the age in which they live.

3. *The "Preterist" View.* Those who hold to the preterist view believe that The Revelation refers to events that were fulfilled in the first century AD, or shortly thereafter. The preterist view holds that all of the events described in The Revelation were fulfilled by the fall of Jerusalem in AD 70, or the fall of Rome in AD 476. To the preterist, the book of Revelation was written primarily to encourage the original readers, and its value for today would therefore be in teaching the value of faithfulness to God.

4. *The "Idealist" View.* This theory says that the book of Revelation does not refer to any specific historical situation but simply presents the principle that good will ultimately triumph over evil. As such, the book is applicable to all Christians at any time, as it is always encouraging to remember the ultimate triumph of good over evil.

Each of these views has merit. Each has its principled proponents. None of them is crazy. But that's not where this book is going. Because, as I hope to make clear in the next few pages, *How to Survive the End of the World* is presented from a vastly different perspective. If you want to know who the Antichrist is or when the Rapture will occur, you will soon be disappointed. But if you want to understand and receive The Revelation in much the same way that its first readers did—and if you're willing to believe that the final book in the Bible may actually have the potential to make your daily life better, fuller, and richer—then keep reading.

In the pages that follow, we are going to study The Revelation with a view to surviving the end of the world . . . *whenever* it may come. We are going to look at the twenty-two chapters of this fascinating book to see if it has value to you, no matter who you are, even if you wouldn't know an apocalypse from an armadillo. And we're going to see if this ancient book can actually prepare us here and now for *whatever* the world and the devil may throw at us.

The Purpose-Driven Book

Not everyone agrees that John the apostle, who wrote the fourth Gospel and three short letters in the New Testament, also wrote The Revelation. But it's quite possible that this was the case, and that, when he wrote the book of Revelation, he was somewhere around ninety years old. One reason I think the Gospel, letters, and The Revelation were all written by the same person is that each of these books contains a clear and straightforward purpose statement.

The Gospel of John says,

> These are written that you may believe that Jesus is the Messiah, the Son of God, and that by believing you may have life in his name.[7]

Similar words appear in the first letter of John in the New Testament:

> I write these things to you who believe in the name of the
> Son of God so that you may know that you have eternal
> life.[8]

In much the same way, the first words of the Bible's last book define it as

> The revelation of Jesus Christ, which God gave him to
> show his servants what must soon take place.[9]

This characteristic is not a common feature of other Bible books, by any means. It not only ties these books together and suggests a common authorship, it also gives us a clear indication of the author's purpose in writing.

Many people have observed a common phenomenon of the latter years in life. When a person reaches an advanced age, it is not unusual for him or her to experience a new clarity of purpose and priority. Time is short. Eternity approaches. At such times, a person tends to focus on what's truly important.

I think that's what is happening in The Revelation. John is in the last years of his life. His time is limited. He cannot know how much longer he will able to think or write clearly. So when the living Christ appears to him in a vision and tells him to write, he focuses on the important, the essential. And I believe he writes to help his brothers and sisters survive the coming apocalypse.

I also believe his message is as current as it is ancient. I believe even his first words will very quickly give us three powerful instructions— immediate applications—that will not only help us survive the end of the world when it comes but will also pay huge dividends if we apply them to our daily lives now.

Feel Blessed

The first message of The Revelation is: feel blessed.

Shocking, I know. That's not the sense a person gets from most "end times" or "last days" books, sermons, movies, or messages. From Sydney

Watson's novels in the 1920s[10] to John Hagee's preaching in the early twenty-first century, the central theme of most messages seems to be "feel scared" or "feel depressed" or "feel panicked." But that is not the message of The Revelation.

Sure, there are some scary things in its twenty-two chapters. There is famine, blood, war, pestilence—it's not a romantic comedy, that's for sure. But it's not a horror movie, either, despite how it has often been interpreted and portrayed that way. It is meant to bless whoever reads it and takes it to heart. Look at the first verses of this unique book:

> The revelation of Jesus Christ, which God gave him to show his servants what must soon take place. He made it known by sending his angel to his servant John, who testifies to everything he saw—that is, the word of God and the testimony of Jesus Christ. Blessed is the one who reads the words of this prophecy, and blessed are those who hear it and take to heart what is written in it, because the time is near.[11]

Now, notice that John refers to this book as "the revelation of Jesus Christ," in verse 1 and as "this prophecy" in verse 3. "Revelation" is the translation of the word *apokalupsis* in Greek. It means, literally, "unveiling."

Notice, too, what it unveils or reveals: "of Jesus Christ." This is not The Revelation of St. John the Divine, as some older versions of the Bible title this book. It is a revelation of Jesus—who he is and what he wants us to know. But it is a prophecy, too, because it is intended (as v. 1 says) "to show his servants what must soon take place."

And then verse 3 tells us,

> Blessed is the one who reads the words of this prophecy, and blessed are those who hear it and take to heart what is written in it, because the time is near.[12]

The mention of "the one who reads" and "those who hear" indicates that John intended this scroll he was writing to be read aloud in public, in the gatherings of the churches in his area of the world. Maybe he envisioned this revelation gaining a wider audience, as his earlier writings had (the Gospel of John, etc.), but he clearly imagined that his first audience would be the person who read his words aloud and the church folk who had gathered to hear it. But that is not the most important point I ask you to notice. The most important realization that should come to us out of Revelation 1:3 is this: We are supposed to be *blessed* by these words. We are intended to take them to heart and be blessed.

As a pastor who has preached from The Revelation, I know that's not a common expectation. In fact, people have often told me that this book scares them. Some have confessed that it has given them nightmares. But that is not how it's supposed to be. The purpose of this book is to *bless* us.

You may read other parts of the Bible to be blessed. You may find blessing in reading the Psalms. You may go to the Gospels to be blessed or to the stories of the patriarchs or David. But, believe it or not, Jesus intends for the words of this revelation to bless you, too. Not scare you—bless you.

Paul the Apostle, after writing to Christians on the other side of the Aegean from Ephesus and Patmos in Thessalonica, about Jesus' Second Coming, said, .

Therefore encourage each other with these words.[13]

"Encourage" one another with his words about the end of the world as we know it, Paul said. The information was meant to be encouraging, not depressing or frightening. The news about "what must soon take place" should not be disturbing or troubling or scary to us. It is given to us to bless us.

So . . . feel blessed. Get ready to be blessed. Plan to be blessed as you read this book. *Look* for blessing in its pages. And don't stop looking until you *get it.*

If we study The Revelation and we are not blessed by it, we have missed its meaning. We have missed the purpose for which Jesus gave it to John, the purpose for which John recorded it, and the purpose for which the Holy Spirit has preserved it through all the intervening centuries since then.

Focus on Jesus

The bulk of The Revelation's first chapter is not about John, who received this revelation, nor about us, who read it, nor *even* about the things which "must soon take place."

It's about Jesus. Look at verses 4–16 with me, and I think you will see what I mean:

> John,
> To the seven churches in the province of Asia:
> Grace and peace to you from him who is, and who was, and who is to come, and from the seven spirits before his throne, and from Jesus Christ, who is the faithful witness, the firstborn from the dead, and the ruler of the kings of the earth.
> To him who loves us and has freed us from our sins by his blood, and has made us to be a kingdom and priests to serve his God and Father—to him be glory and power for ever and ever! Amen.
>
> *"Look, he is coming with the clouds,"*
> *and "every eye will see him,*
> *even those who pierced him";*
> *and all the peoples of the earth "will mourn because of him."*
> *So shall it be! Amen.*
>
> "I am the Alpha and the Omega," says the Lord God, "who is, and who was, and who is to come, the Almighty."

I, John, your brother and companion in the suffering and kingdom and patient endurance that are ours in Jesus, was on the island of Patmos because of the word of God and the testimony of Jesus.

On the Lord's Day I was in the Spirit, and I heard behind me a loud voice like a trumpet, which said: "Write on a scroll what you see and send it to the seven churches: to Ephesus, Smyrna, Pergamum, Thyatira, Sardis, Philadelphia and Laodicea."

I turned around to see the voice that was speaking to me. And when I turned I saw seven golden lampstands, and among the lampstands was someone like a son of man, dressed in a robe reaching down to his feet and with a golden sash around his chest. His head and hair were white like wool, as white as snow, and his eyes were like blazing fire. His feet were like bronze glowing in a furnace, and his voice was like the sound of rushing waters. In his right hand he held seven stars, and out of his mouth came a sharp double-edged sword. His face was like the sun shining in all its brilliance.[14]

Most people, it seems, study the book of Revelation to learn secrets. "Who is the Antichrist?" "What does the number of the beast mean?" "Is Russia Gog and China Magog?" It can be fascinating stuff, I grant you, but that is not the purpose of this book, because that is not the purpose of The Revelation. And if we come to the study of The Revelation *without* focusing on Jesus, that may well show us how badly we *need* the message of this book.

He is the one who is, and who was, and who is to come,
he is the faithful witness,
the firstborn from the dead,
the ruler of the kings of the earth.

He is the one who loves us and has freed us from our sins
by his blood,
and made us to be a kingdom and priests to serve his God
and Father—
He is coming with the clouds,
and every eye will see him.
He is the Alpha and the Omega,
and every knee will bow before him.

Few of us really grasp what the phrase, "the Alpha and the Omega"
means. It harks back to the two epics of the Greek poet Homer, the
Iliad and the *Odyssey*. Some of us read them in high school. Others
of us read the *Cliff's Notes*. I may or may not have skipped class the
day that test was scheduled.

But to someone in the world of John's day, which was saturated with
and dominated by Greek culture, the *Iliad* and the *Odyssey* were as influential as the Internet is in our day. And the Greek understanding was
that, if a god was named in the *Iliad* or the *Odyssey*, that god was real
. . . and worthy of worship. Any god that was *not* named in Homer was
irrelevant.

The standard Homerian text was compiled by Alexandrian scholars,
who organized the *Iliad* and the *Odyssey* into twenty-four separate books
and labeled each book with one of the twenty-four letters of the Greek
alphabet—from alpha, the first letter, to omega, the last.

So when Jesus reveals himself to John, and to us, as the Alpha and
Omega, he is referring not only to the Greek alphabet, but also to *every
god* in the Greek and Roman pantheon of gods. He is saying, in effect,
"You can TOSS OUT your *Iliad* and *Odyssey*. You can THROW AWAY
every god Homer mentions. You can RENOUNCE every god in every
temple in every land—THEY ARE NOT GODS! I AM THE ALPHA
AND THE OMEGA. . . .

I AM the catalog of the divine,
I AM the KING of KINGS and LORD of LORDS,

I AM over all, and through all, and in all."

John saw him in a form "like a son of man," dressed in a robe reaching down to his feet, with a golden sash around his chest, with head and hair white like wool, white as snow, and eyes blazing like fire. His feet were like bronze glowing in a furnace, and his voice was like the sound of a mighty waterfall. In his right hand he held seven stars, out of his mouth came a sharp double-edged sword, and his face was like the sun shining in all its brilliance.

This is Jesus. This is your Jesus. This is the One giving the revelation. Your friend, your Savior, your confidante, your protector, provider, redeemer, healer, and help. Your king.

This is the Revealer. Knowing him, can you fear the future?

This is his message. Seeing him, what can hurt you?

These are his words. Having him, can you worry about the coming apocalypse?

Do you *have* him? Is he yours? Is he alive in your life? Is he ruling over your heart?

Because that is nearly the first thing John shows us in this revelation. Because you can't focus on Jesus until you find him . . . and when you focus on him, all the trials and tribulations, all the worries and fears, all the stresses and strains of this life come into perspective, and lose their power.

I hope you know him. And if you don't, I hope you'll be quick, in this moment, before reading further, to breathe a prayer of confession, surrender, and commitment to him (turn to pp. 207–8 for a suggested prayer to help you). Otherwise, there is no blessing or comfort in the words that follow. But with him as your Savior and king, with him as your focus, all that is to come can be the best of all possible futures for you.

Feel His Touch

Maybe you noticed. Maybe not. But back in verse 12 of the passage we looked at earlier, John writes something odd, something incongruent. Did you catch it? He said,

> I turned around to see the voice that was speaking to me.[15]

I turned around to see the voice. To see . . . the voice.

Did you notice that?

You can't *see* a voice. You *hear* a voice, right? You don't *see* it.

Maybe he was just being careless. Maybe he gave his proofreader the day off. But I don't think so. That would be out of character for him, based on the proficiency and care that is elsewhere evident in his writings.

No, I think something else is going on.

I think the voice of Jesus was so tangible to him, so real, so substantial, that he expected it to be visible, to have form. And, indeed, the vision of Jesus that met his eyes when he turned was even more than he expected. The following verses say,

> When I saw him, I fell at his feet as though dead. Then he placed his right hand on me and said: "Do not be afraid. I am the First and the Last. I am the Living One; I was dead, and behold I am alive for ever and ever! And I hold the keys of death and Hades.
>
> "Write, therefore, what you have seen, what is now and what will take place later. The mystery of the seven stars that you saw in my right hand and of the seven golden lampstands is this: The seven stars are the angels of the seven churches, and the seven lampstands are the seven churches."[16]

As you will see in the rest of the book of Revelation, there is a lot going on in those few verses. There are many layers and levels of symbolism and significance in those words. There is so much we could study and meditate on.

But we won't. Because the central message is so powerful, we can't risk missing it. Those verses depict something you want. Something you need. No matter who you are.

They depict something I want for you, too . . . and for me.

Because, notice, when John saw this Jesus,

his face like the sun,
his eyes like fire,
his feet like bronze,
his voice like the sound of a waterfall,

he fell on his face . . . as any one of us would do in the presence of such power. But look what happened next:

> he placed his right hand on me and said: "Do not be afraid."[17]

He placed his right hand on John and said: "Do not be afraid." He touched him. Gently, we may infer. Reassuringly. And he spoke tender words of comfort to him.

Wouldn't that be nice? Wouldn't you like to have that, too? What if you could feel that touch? Hear those words?

You may not be afraid. Or you may not know that you're afraid. But what if now—and for the remainder of your life—you could feel Jesus' right hand on you? What if you could sleep and wake, walk and work, laugh and cry with the awareness that his hand is on your life? What if you could face the future—whatever it holds—without being afraid?

I don't know why you picked up this book. I don't know why you're still reading. You have your own reasons. They may be reasons that are unrelated to my aims in writing. But I believe that, in God's wisdom and love, he will meet you here, in these pages. I believe he *is* meeting you here, to place his right hand on you and say, "Do not be afraid."

Before you read any further or do anything else, will you give him that chance? Close your eyes, close this book, and be still for a few moments, waiting for his hand and for his voice.

Prayer

Lord Jesus, you are my friend, my Savior, my confidante, protector, provider, redeemer, healer, and help. You are my king. Because I know you, I do not fear the future.

Because you are with me, what can hurt me? Because you are mine and I am yours, I will not worry about the things that are to come.

I bow to you, Lord. Touch me with your hand. Help me to hear your voice, and experience the blessing you intend for me through the coming pages. Amen.

3

Have a Little Talk with Jesus

Now let us have a little talk with Jesus,
Let us tell him all about our troubles,
He will hear our faintest cry,
He will answer by and by
> —Cleavant Derricks

People say goodbye to their kids all the time. Especially after they've graduated, grown up, enlisted, or married. Parents know it's coming. They've planned and prepared for it for years. You'd think they'd be ready. Turns out, not so much.

My son had graduated from high school, had worked, and had taken a few college courses locally, when he was accepted to a school a thousand miles away, in sunny Florida. My wife the lovely Robin and I packed a minivan full of necessities for school, such as hundreds of music CDs and a PS2 and GameCube, and headed south on a Sunday afternoon. That morning at church had been filled with tearful hugs and goodbyes from family and friends who acted as though they would never see him again.

After two days of driving, we moved him into the apartment he would share with another student who had graduated from the same high school. We stocked the refrigerator and pantry and made sure the maintenance man fixed the clogged kitchen drain before we left. I slipped him some money when my wife wasn't looking. She did the same. Then we hugged him long and hard and said goodbye.

I thought my heart would explode. Or my head, from holding in tears.

The first few hours of our return drive passed in silence. It felt like someone had died. We knew we'd be in touch, of course. We had phones. He had a phone. We could email each other. And we knew we'd be sending care packages with homemade baked goods and other items. But he was leaving, and none of us knew for sure when he'd be back.

The distance never got shorter. The separation never got easier. But, in the coming months, I found some comfort and reward in writing letters to my son. Real letters. On real stationery. Letters in which I said to him many of the things that were in my heart but that don't always get said in the come-and-go of daily life. I tried to tell him how much I loved him and how proud I was of him. I wrote about my fondest memories of him and what I hoped he remembered of me. I did my best to encourage him, comfort him, and cheer him. And I took every opportunity to urge him onward not only toward graduation but toward a godly manhood. I don't know if he kept those letters, but I made copies of them. And I still have them.

Those letters were not my last words to my son. In fact, he and his wife and two children now live just a dozen miles from my home. But his time away at school in Florida did provide me with an opportunity to write some things to him that I hope had an influence and made a difference.

What sorts of things would you write to your loved ones in such a case? What would you say if you were to write down the most important things you want your loved ones to know? To do? To remember?

Once you answer those questions, here's a few more: Why don't you do it? What are you waiting for? What prevents you from saying—NOW—the things you want most for the people you care about?

Special Delivery

Letter-writing is fast becoming a lost art, thanks to cell phones and Skype, email and text messaging. We just don't write—or receive—letters much anymore. When was the last time you received a letter—a real letter, not a newsletter or card, but a letter—from a friend or family member? See what I mean?

In fact, led by Hawaii and Indiana in 2011, many state departments of education in the United States have stopped requiring schools to teach cursive handwriting. They say technology has changed the way people communicate to such an extent that students will no longer need that particular skill. Handwriting, they say, is being replaced with typing and texting.

I think it's sad. While I welcome all forms of communication from those I love, there will always be something special about receiving a handwritten note or letter. It conveys personality in a way typed missives do not and suggests a level of personal involvement—commitment, even—that emoticons lack.

For this reason, I wish the second and third chapters of The Revelation given to John on the island of Patmos could have been preserved for us in their original form. Not that most of us could read the letters or understand the language. But it is utterly crucial for us to recognize that, right at the outset of this strange and wonderful collection of visions and messages that come to us as the last book in the Christian Scriptures, a series of specific and heartfelt letters introduces everything that follows. They are seven separate letters to seven specific churches. But, unlike much of the New Testament, these letters were not written by apostles like Paul, John, or Peter. These letters came from Jesus Christ himself. They were dictated to John, the man many scholars agree is the "Beloved Disciple" of the fourth Gospel, and they were intended for specific churches in actual towns throughout an area that today is western Turkey.

First Words on Last Things

The seven churches Jesus addressed in the seven letters that now appear in what we know as Revelation 2 and 3 are the same seven churches for which the entire revelation was intended. It is introduced as follows:

> The revelation of Jesus Christ, which God gave him to show to his servants the things that must soon take place. He made it known by sending his angel to his servant John, who bore witness to the word of God and to the testimony of Jesus

Christ, even to all that he saw. Blessed is the one who reads aloud the words of this prophecy, and blessed are those who hear, and who keep what is written in it, for the time is near.

John to the seven churches that are in Asia:

Grace to you and peace from him who is and who was and who is to come. . . .

I, John, your brother and partner in the tribulation and the kingdom and the patient endurance that are in Jesus, was on the island called Patmos on account of the word of God and the testimony of Jesus. I was in the Spirit on the Lord's day, and I heard behind me a loud voice like a trumpet saying, "Write what you see in a book and send it to the seven churches, to Ephesus and to Smyrna and to Pergamum and to Thyatira and to Sardis and to Phila-delphia and to Laodicea."[18]

The Revelation was written specifically for seven churches that were located in cities found along the major Roman trade road through that part of the world, like the interstate freeways of our day or the railroads of an earlier time. Travelers and traders would have reached each city in the same order in which they are named, roughly thirty miles (a full day's journey on foot) between each one.

There were almost certainly very practical reasons this revelation was addressed to those particular cities, and not to, say, Rome or Jerusalem. They were nearby. They were on the trade route. And they were, starting with Ephesus, the churches that were very likely under John's pastoral influence, even when he was in exile. But there was probably another reason.

Multiple Choice

Chapter Two discussed four main approaches Bible scholars and students take when trying to understand and interpret The Revelation.

Similarly, there are four main ways people try to understand these letters from Jesus to the seven churches of Asia Minor:

1. *The immediate application.* One possible view of these letters is that Jesus gave these messages to John for these specific first-century churches, and that's it—no more. In that case, their main value to us is in learning from these churches' example.

2. *The universal application.* That is, that these seven churches signify the whole church, in every age, and thus Jesus' message to *each* church applies to us, right here, right now. Maybe some more, maybe some less, but this view is that Jesus is giving these words to us not merely as examples but as a message for today.

3. *The chronological application.* Some scholars and students believe these seven letters depict seven ages of church history, from the first seventy years of church history depicted in the letter to the church in Ephesus, to the current age, the twentieth century on, which looks like the seventh letter to the church at Laodicea.

4. *The individual application.* Some have suggested that these seven letters might portray the blessings and temptations of the Christian life in seven phases, from the moment a person is freshly saved from sin and reconciled to God (the letter to Ephesus) to the moment when that person has become weary and lukewarm in his or her Christian walk (the letter to Laodicea).

Those aren't the only possible ways to understand Revelation 2–3, of course. And it's even feasible that "all of the above" are true. After all, the Bible's message sometimes runs several layers deep.

But our approach in this book will be a little different. As Hebrews 4:12 tells us, "The Word of God is living and active." The Bible was never meant to be simply a source of intellectual exercise or passive theological epiphanies that make us feel smarter than before. It is a force that penetrates and delves deep into us and activates action. The point of studying the Bible is not merely to learn things you've never heard of before but to experience God in a way you've never known before and then to live in a way nobody has ever seen before.

Return Address

Notice that seven churches are named in the first few chapters of The Revelation. Seven distinct churches in seven different cities. You will notice, as we study this amazing book, that numbers will play a significant part. They are used for symbolic purposes throughout The Revelation, and that is certainly the case in these early chapters. The number seven is no accident. The number seven in the Bible is widely acknowledged as the number of completeness, or perfection, symbolically speaking.

Eugene Peterson, in his book on The Revelation, *Reversed Thunder*, points out,

> The second-century Muratorian canon observed that both St. Paul and St. John wrote letters to seven churches. Seven churches summarize all churches.[19]

Remember, the purpose of The Revelation is to be a blessing to anyone who reads and takes it to heart, and to prepare that person for the future—the things that "must soon take place."[20] So, what if we read these seven letters not only as Jesus' words to those first-century believers but also as a guide to us, part of Jesus' enduring message for surviving the end of the world? What if we receive those seven letters much as my son received my notes to him when he was away in college—as urgent, heartfelt encouragements for how to live through a crucial phase of our lives?

After an initial greeting in each of these letters, Jesus identifies himself with a descriptive phrase, a phrase that is particular to each specific church. To the Ephesian church, he refers to himself as

him who holds the seven stars in his right hand and walks among the seven golden lampstands.[21]

To the church at Smyrna, he calls himself

the First and the Last, who died and came to life again.[22]

To the church at Pergamum, he makes himself known as

him who has the sharp, double-edged sword.[23]

To his followers in Thyatira, he is

the Son of God, whose eyes are like blazing fire and whose feet are like burnished bronze.[24]

To those at Sardis:

him who holds the seven spirits of God and the seven stars.[25]

To the Philadelphian church:

him who is holy and true, who hold the key of David.[26]

And to the Laodiceans:

the Amen, the faithful and true witness, the ruler of God's creation.[27]

Seems curious, if you ask me. He could have just said, "I'm Jesus." He could have used the same identifying phrase to each church. Maybe, "The Risen Lord." Or, as John called him in chapter 1, "The One who is, who was, and who is to come." They would have gotten the point, right?

But he didn't. He identified himself to each church in a unique way. Why? I think it is because a personal, unique encounter with Jesus is absolutely crucial to the task of preparing for the end of the world. None of us should think or feel himself ready for the end of the world until he has consciously encountered the living, risen Jesus Christ and personally experienced his grace, forgiveness, salvation, and resurrection power. If you're reading this book and that doesn't describe you, then let me once more invite you to turn to pages 207–8 for a suggested prayer to guide you in making sure the Risen Lord of Revelation is also a living reality in your heart and life.

End-of-the-World Imperatives

After the greeting and the description of Jesus in each letter, there follows in each case the Greek word *oida* . . . "I know." That's an important phrase to focus and meditate on if you hope to survive the end of the world. Jesus knows. He knows you. He knows where you live. He knows the best and the worst about you. He knows what you're facing. He knows where you're failing and ways in which you're improving. He knows.

Jesus told the seven churches in chapters 2 and 3 of The Revelation the things he knew about them. In all but two cases, he affirmed something good, something praiseworthy. For example, he praised the church in Ephesus for their untiring work and perseverance and Smyrna for their brave suffering. He commended the people in Pergamum for courageous witness and those in Thyatira for their growth, progress, and perseverance. He told the church in ancient Philadelphia that he had taken notice of their steadfastness.

Jesus also mentioned to five of the seven churches the things he saw that did not please him, things in need of correction. Ephesus had abandoned their first love. Pergamum had been indifferent to false teaching. The church in Thyatira was tolerant of immorality, those in Sardis were apathetic, and the Laodiceans, famously, were lukewarm and complacent. And to each of the churches, he commanded a change and promised a reward.

But there is more to it than that. The challenges faced by those seven churches have not disappeared from the earth. Their strengths and weaknesses are no less common among twenty-first-century Christians than they were in the Apostle John's day. And for more than twenty centuries now, much of the church has agreed that Jesus' message to those seven churches was not for them alone. So it is not hard to imagine that part of Jesus' plan in sending those messages through John to the seven churches was to give us—today—some key attitudes or actions to carry us to victory as the end of the world approaches.

In fact, it is possible to identify twelve end-of-the-world imperatives for us, today, in those letters to the churches in Ephesus, Smyrna, Pergamum, Thyatira, Sardis, Philadelphia, and Laodicea. The Lord's commendations and corrections to those seven churches may actually provide a succinct guide for anyone who wants to be ready for the end of the world when it comes.

Guard against Evil

Jesus' first letter, dictated to John for the church at Ephesus (John's home church), commended the Ephesians for guarding against evil. He says,

> I know your deeds, your hard work and your perseverance. I know that you cannot tolerate wicked people, that you have tested those who claim to be apostles but are not, and have found them false.[28]

Decades before giving this message to the Ephesians, Jesus had warned his first disciples that as the end of the world approaches,

> False messiahs and false prophets will appear and perform great signs and wonders to deceive, if possible, even the elect.[29]

The twenty-first century is not different from the first century in that respect. Those who hope to survive the end of the world must guard against evil. We must not tolerate wicked people. We must "not believe every spirit, but test the spirits to see whether they are from God, because many false prophets have gone out into the world."[30] If anything, our task may be harder than our first-century predecessors in the faith. Through modern media—books, television, radio, podcasts, Websites, and so on—more teachers and preachers, both orthodox and heretical, enter our lives than ever before in human history. We must be wise and discerning. We must be careful to whom and to what we listen. We must not believe someone simply because they have a successful television ministry or a best-selling book. Now, more than ever, we must measure every message and every messenger against the Word of God and not dismiss sin or error because we happen to like someone or because they happen to be famous. We must guard against evil.

Persevere in Hardship

Jesus' commendation to the church at Ephesus goes on:

> You have persevered and have endured hardships for my name, and have not grown weary.[31]

It was not easy to be a follower of Jesus in the first century at Ephesus (or anywhere in the world of that time). Christ-followers faced political persecution, economic discrimination, social exclusion, and more. The same is true for many in the twenty-first century, as Christians face church bombings in Nigeria, confiscation of property in Malaysia, imprisonment in Iran, and violent riots in India.

You may not have such hardships. But your circumstances may call for patient endurance, nonetheless: Illness. Unemployment. Aging parents. Wayward children. Your hardships may not be a consequence of your Christian commitment, as were the Ephesians', but the call to perseverance is the same. Faithful, persevering obedience ("a long obedience in the same direction," to borrow Friedrich Nietzsche's phrase) is necessary for anyone who hopes to survive the end of the world.

Rekindle Your First Love

Jesus' words to the church at Ephesus were not all positive. After praising them for guarding against evil and persevering through hardship, he says,

> Yet I hold this against you: You have forsaken the love you had at first. Consider how far you have fallen! Repent and do the things you did at first.[32]

Thirty or more years earlier, the Apostle Paul had written to the Ephesians,[33]

> Ever since I heard about your faith in the Lord Jesus and your love for all God's people, I have not stopped giving thanks for you.[34]

Apparently, the ardor of their early Christian experience, the loving enthusiasm they shared with the Lord Jesus and everyone around them, had cooled by the time Jesus dictated his letter to the Apostle John on the island of Patmos.

It can happen to anyone. It *does* happen, all the time. Time goes by, life goes on, and even the most vibrant, loving heart can grow cold. That is why these verses are given to us, to remind us to re-kindle *our* first love, to reignite the fires of devotion to God and love for each other that too easily and too soon dwindle and die.

The Lord even tells us clearly and succinctly how it's done, how to reclaim our early experience: remember, repent, and repeat. Remember the heights of joy and love from which we have fallen, repent and find forgiveness and "do the things you did at first." Have I neglected prayer since those halcyon days? Did I spend more time at the feet of Jesus then? Am I neglecting worship? Do I hoard my blessings instead of sharing them? If I'm going to survive the end of the world, I'm going to do it by rekindling my first love, as Jesus urged on the church at Ephesus.

Don't Fear the Future

In spite of the many strange and mysterious images described in the revelation Jesus gave to his servant John, I nonetheless find it odd (and sad) that it is, to many, a frightening vision. After all, not only did the Lord promise a message intended to bless all those who receive it, he also explicitly urged against fear of the future. In the second letter of The Revelation, he addresses the church at Smyrna, saying,

> I know your afflictions and your poverty—yet you are rich! I know about the slander of those who say they are Jews and are not, but are a synagogue of Satan. Do not be afraid of what you are about to suffer. I tell you, the devil will put some of you in prison to test you, and you will suffer perse-cution for ten days. Be faithful, even to the point of death, and I will give you life as your victor's crown.[35]

"Do not be afraid of what you are about to suffer." To be fair, none of us likes to suffer. And I have to admit, if I opened a letter that told me I am about to suffer—maybe even to the point of death—I would probably have to sit down. I might get a little queasy about that prospect. Wouldn't you?

But Jesus tells those people—who are already suffering some affliction, poverty, and slander—not to be afraid of the future. He even tells them their persecution will last "ten days," which is open to many intriguing explanations but seems intended to encourage them with the news that their persecution will not go on forever.

But what do the Lord's words to the church at Smyrna do for us, today? To those of us who see the end of all things approaching, I believe the Lord's message is the same: Don't fear the future. Don't get all wrapped up in conspiracy theories and ominous scenarios. Don't tremble, triumph. Focus your efforts on being faithful, no matter what comes your way, and in a relatively short amount of time, you will be rewarded far beyond whatever pain you've had to suffer.

Cling to Christ

The Lord's letter to his church at Smyrna is followed by the letter to the church at Pergamum, a city which rivaled Ephesus and Smyrna for power and prestige.[36] To his followers there, Jesus writes:

> I know where you live—where Satan has his throne. Yet you remain true to my name. You did not renounce your faith in me, not even in the days of Antipas, my faithful witness, who was put to death in your city—where Satan lives.[37]

Idolatry pervaded Pergamum, and the city may have been the birthplace of Roman emperor worship. Yet, in spite of the tremendous pressures to accommodate and imitate the surrounding culture, the church there clung faithfully to Jesus Christ—even when one of their number (possibly their pastor) was martyred.

You may feel at times as though Satan has established his throne in your city (or neighborhood, workplace, or school). You may feel outnumbered and outgunned. You may even have grieved as your brothers and sisters have paid dearly for their faithfulness to Jesus Christ. But his word to you is the same as his word to the church at Pergamum: Cling to him. Give no ground. No compromise. No surrender.

Whatever it takes, hold on to Jesus. Not to tradition. Not to religion. Not to popular opinion. Cling to Jesus. Hang on to him . . . for dear life.

Learn from the Past

A number of dear friends of mine have heard the dreaded news from a doctor, informing them that they have only so long to live. One died within a few weeks. Another lingered for a year. Still another is still breathing, working, laughing, and exercising more than five years after a surgeon told him he had less than a year to live.

Some people, on hearing such news, become energized and try to squeeze as much life as they can into the time they have left. Others wax nostalgic, reviewing and reliving the past. Something similar can take place for those who anticipate the end of the world. But the rest of the letter to the church at Pergamum provides an excellent insight into the proper way to view the past in light of the future.

After commending his followers in Pergamum for their faithfulness, Jesus goes on:

> Nevertheless, I have a few things against you: There are some among you who hold to the teaching of Balaam, who taught Balak to entice the Israelites to sin so that they ate food sacrificed to idols and committed sexual immorality. Likewise, you also have those who hold to

the teaching of the Nicolaitans. Repent therefore! Otherwise, I will soon come to you and will fight against them with the sword of my mouth.[38]

Decades before this message was delivered through John, the first leaders of the church met in Jerusalem to decide how to deal with the challenge of Gentiles—who knew little or nothing of the law of God—becoming Christ-followers. That church council agreed that Gentile Christians, like their Jewish brothers and sisters in Christ, should "abstain from food polluted by idols, from sexual immorality, from the meat of strangled animals and from blood."[39] Now, however, some in the church at Pergamum had disregarded that apostolic teaching and were repeating past errors. They had failed to learn from the past and so were subject to correction.

Some things never change. We still tend to compromise with an idolatrous culture. We continue to be tempted by sexual immorality. We fall into behaviors because those around us are doing it. No matter how often the consequences play out like a morality play, we too often repeat the tragic mistakes of the past. So Jesus says to us, as he said to his followers in Pergamum, "Repent." Turn and go a different direction. Be warned by the errors and sins of Balaam, Samson, David, Judas, Peter, and others. Use history—ancient and modern—to inform and guide your future.

Love and Serve Others

A former U.S. intelligence officer living in Idaho hosts a blog[40] that has attracted millions of hits. The site recommends getting your "beans, bullets, and Band-Aids together" in preparation for TEOTWAWKI—the end of the world as we know it. The blog's header bills it as "the daily Web log for prepared individuals living in uncertain times."

Any time expectations of the end of the world rise, people naturally wonder if they should stockpile necessities and be prepared to defend their stores against robbery or confiscation. Such an approach, however, is contrary to the spirit of Christ, who commends the church at Thyatira with these words:

> I know your deeds, your love and faith, your service and perseverance, and that you are now doing more than you did at first.[41]

Surviving TEOTWAWKI, according to Jesus, does not require stockpiles of "beans, bullets, and Band-Aids." It calls for an overflow of love and service to others. Whatever others may do when the Apocalypse is now, I want to be known for my love and faith, my service and perseverance. I want to be doing more then than I ever did before.

One of the best preparations we can make for "the end of the world as we know it" is to love more, give more, help more, and serve more than we have in the past.

Don't Tolerate Falsehood

My dear friend was on her deathbed. She knew she was dying, and, though she didn't want to leave her children and other loved ones, she was ready for deliverance from her disease-wracked body and into the presence of Jesus. While she still had strength, however, she used it well. Her bedroom became an anteroom of heaven. She met with people—those she had asked to see and others who had come to visit on their own initiative. And to those people, she didn't mince words. She spoke lovingly, but bluntly.

She had known some of those people for many years. They had talked many times. But never as pointedly and purposefully as in her final days. She knew her time was limited. And there was no time for falsehood, no time for skirting the truth. No time for anything but the business of heaven.

Those are the days we live in, too. In the message Jesus gave to the church at Thyatira, he made it clear that in the last days his people should not tolerate falsehood or skirt the truth. He says:

Nevertheless, I have this against you: You tolerate that woman Jezebel, who calls herself a prophet. By her teaching she misleads my servants into sexual immorality and the eating of food sacrificed to idols. I have given her time to repent of her immorality, but she is unwilling. So I will cast her on a bed of suffering, and I will make those who commit adultery with her suffer intensely, unless they repent of her ways. I will strike her children dead. Then all the churches will know that I am he who searches hearts and minds, and I will repay each of you according to your deeds.[42]

We don't know who this "Jezebel" woman was. The name is symbolic, of course, referring to the evil queen of Israel, the wife of Ahab. But whoever she was, this woman was misleading the people of Thyatira in much the same ways the people of Pergamum were being misled. And Jesus made it clear that his followers should not tolerate such deception and falsehood.

The issues we face today may be different, but the time is even shorter. Those who would survive the end of the world cannot afford to tolerate falsehood. We must not participate in gossip, slander, and lies. We should have no patience for the silly (and harmful) games some people play. "Hate what is evil; cling to what is good."[43]

Awaken from Slumber

Jesus has no praise for the church in Sardis, only a warning:

I know your deeds; you have a reputation of being alive, but you are dead. Wake up! Strengthen what remains and is about to die, for I have found your deeds unfinished in the sight of my God. Remember, therefore, what you have received and heard; hold it fast, and repent. But if you do not wake up, I will come like a thief, and you will not know at what time I will come to you.[44]

My son Aaron is the soundest sleeper I've ever known. Once he gets to sleep, he is extremely difficult to awaken. He and I recently shared a laugh as we remembered my efforts to wake him for school when he was a young teenager. The alarm in his bedroom would awaken *me*, and I would stagger into his room, turn it off, and shake him awake. He would sit up on his bed and, as soon as I left the room, lie down again. I would come back, rouse him, and insist that he stand up and get dressed. If I left the room, he would lie down again. This tragicomic routine would often repeat itself many times before he stumbled his way into school—where he would continue to doze through most of the morning.

That is a picture of many church folk. For all appearances, we're alive. We go to church. We don't smoke, or chew, or hang around with those who do. We say grace at mealtimes. But our deeds are unfinished. There is no pulse. No passion. We are going through the motions, but there's no *life* in our "Christian life." The message of Jesus to the church at Sardis is a reveille call. It summons us not only to wake up but to do calisthenics ("strengthen what remains") and dress for battle.

What will awaken you? What will arouse your passion? What will it take to get you up from your cot and out into the battle? Maybe you know, maybe you don't. But, whatever it takes, don't settle for sleep when the King calls you to combat.

Seize Your God-Given Opportunities

The church in Philadelphia was probably a small group of Christ-followers who had little going for them compared to the other churches Jesus addressed; he referred to them as having "little strength." But despite their "little strength," Jesus had only praise—and many promises—for this church. He says,

> I know your deeds. See, I have placed before you an open
> door that no one can shut. I know that you have little

strength, yet you have kept my word and have not denied my name.[45]

No one is really sure exactly what "open door" Jesus referred to. Some think it was a door to ministry, like Paul mentions in 1 Corinthians 16:9. Others think it's the door to heaven or a door of escape from persecution, especially since, in verse 10, Jesus promises to keep them "from the hour of trial that is going to come on the whole world to test the inhabitants of the earth."[46]

It doesn't really matter. The point, for our purposes, is this: when Jesus opens a door, we need to go through it. When we are presented with a clearly God-given opportunity, we ought to seize it. This is one of the reasons to make sure we're fully awake, as Jesus commanded the church at Sardis—because we need to be on our toes, spiritually speaking, to recognize and capitalize on any door God opens.

So, what door is God opening for you? What opportunity has he placed before you? Sure, it may be frightening. It may involve risk. It may take courage to walk through it. But remember, time is short. The end is near. And if God opens it, no man can shut it.

Take a Stand

The most famous letter of Jesus to a church is, of course, the letter to the Laodiceans. He writes:

I know your deeds, that you are neither cold nor hot. I wish you were either one or the other! So, because you are lukewarm—neither hot nor cold—I am about to spit you out of my mouth.[47]

It is a vivid picture Jesus paints. Imagine lifting a cup to your mouth, expecting fresh hot coffee and tasting something tepid instead. Or taking a sip from a straw on a hot summer day, anticipating ice-cold lemonade but getting a tart mouthful at room temperature. What would you do? Depending on where you are at the time, you might turn your head and spit it out.

Jesus says the people of the Laodicean church are lukewarm like that. They are not holy, but at least they are not heretics. They are neither greedy nor generous. They cause no offense, but neither do they stir anyone to action. They are comfortable. Content. Complacent.

Jesus reserves a special disdain for those who are lukewarm in the last days. He is repulsed by them. Disgusted. Sickened. Nauseated. He calls such people "wretched, pitiful, poor, blind and naked."[48]

These are not the times to be lukewarm. This is no time to sit on the fence. John R. W. Stott writes:

> One longs to see today robust and courageous men and women bringing to Jesus Christ their thoughtful and total commitment. He asks for this. He even says that if we will not be hot, he would prefer us cold to lukewarm. Better to be frigid than tepid, he implies. His meaning is not far to seek. If he is true; if he is the Son of God who became a human being, died for our sins, and was raised from death; if Christmas Day, Good Friday and Easter Day are more than meaningless anniversaries, then nothing less than our wholehearted commitment to Christ will do. This means that we will put him first in our private and public life, seeking his glory and obeying his will. Better be icy in our indifference or go into active opposition to him than insult him with an insipid compromise which nauseates him![49]

"So be earnest,"[50] Jesus says. "Be zealous."[51] "Be committed."[52] "Be diligent."[53] "Be enthusiastic *and* in earnest *and* burning with zeal."[54]

Keep Company with Jesus

After Jesus' breathtaking rebuke to the church at Laodicea, his tone turns pleading:

> Here I am! I stand at the door and knock. If anyone hears my voice and opens the door, I will come in and eat with that person, and they with me.[55]

These are among the most famous words in Scripture. They have been memorialized in song, depicted in art, and plastered on walls. Men and women of God have taught that verse and preached it and presented it as a nice little invitation to open your heart to Jesus and become "born again." I hate to burst anyone's bubble, but that's not what the verse is about.

It was written to a church, remember? To people who already said "yes" to Jesus. It was not written to skeptics and seekers, but to followers of Jesus who were making him sick. And to those complacent Christians, Jesus said, in effect, "Open up to me. I'm right here. I'm knocking at the door. Let's sit down together. Let's have a meal. Let's keep company with each other."

Brennan Manning writes,

> Sadly, the meaning of meal sharing is largely lost in the Christian community today. In the Near East, to share a meal with someone is a guarantee of peace, trust, fraternity, and forgiveness: the shared table symbolizes a shared life. For an orthodox Jew to say, "I would like to have dinner with you," is a metaphor implying "I would like to enter into friendship with you." Even today an American Jew will share a donut and a cup of coffee with you, but to extend a dinner invitation is to say: "Come to my *mikdash me-at*, the miniature sanctuary of my dining

room table where we will celebrate the most sacred and beautiful experience that life affords—friendship."[56]

As disgusting as the Laodicean church was to Jesus, he made it clear that he wanted to keep company with them. He wanted to share life with them. He wanted to celebrate with them the most sacred and beautiful experience that life affords—friendship. And he wants the same with you, too.

If you truly plan to survive the end of the world, you can do no better than to keep company with Jesus. Don't be content with anything other than a constant, passionate, vibrant friendship with him, because he won't be satisfied with anything less than that with you.

To Survival . . . and Beyond

After his commendations and corrections to each of those seven churches, Jesus issued a promise to every one of them.

To the church in Ephesus, Jesus says,

> "To him who overcomes, I will give the right to eat from the tree of life, which is in the paradise of God."[57]

To the church in Smyrna, he promises the crown of life. To Pergamum, a white stone with a new name on it. To Thyatira, the morning star; to Sardis, white garments; to Philadelphia, he said they would be made a pillar in his temple. And to the Laodiceans, the right to sit on his throne.

Seven is the number of perfection, completeness. And Jesus gave seven unique promises to his followers in Ephesus, Smyrna, Pergamum, Thyatira, Sardis, Philadelphia, and Laodicea—promises not only of survival, but victory, at the last day.

I believe those are not only Jesus' words to those first-century believers but also to us. I believe we can receive those promises much as my son received my notes to him when he was away in college—as urgent, heartfelt encouragements for how to live through a crucial phase of our lives. I believe if we guard against evil, persevere in hardship, rekindle our first love, refuse to fear the future, cling to Christ, learn from the past, love and serve others, reject falsehood, awaken from slumber, seize whatever opportunities God puts in front of us, take a stand, and keep company with Jesus, we will not only survive . . . but triumph in these last days.

Prayer

Lord Jesus, Son of God, First and Last, Alpha and Omega, the Amen, the faithful and true witness, the ruler of God's creation, help me to please you in these last days. Teach me to guard against evil and persevere in hardship. Help me to rekindle my first love. Let me refuse to fear the future and cling closely and completely to you. Lead me to learn from the past, love and serve others, reject falsehood, and awaken from slumber. Help me to seize whatever opportunities you put in front of me. Help me to take a stand. Let me keep company with you, moment by moment, and day by day. Amen.

4

We Fall Down

Holy, holy, holy! All the saints adore Thee,
Casting down their golden crowns around the glassy sea;
Cherubim and seraphim falling down before Thee,
Who was, and is, and evermore shall be.
                                        —Reginald Heber

In 1792, a forty-two-year-old English woman named Joanna Southcott announced that she was the woman described in Revelation 12 as "clothed with the sun, and the moon under her feet, and upon her head a crown of twelve stars."[58] She composed prophecies in rhyme, and in 1814 declared that she was pregnant by immaculate conception (at the age of sixty-four!) with the new Messiah, called "Shiloh" in the book of Genesis.[59] Though she never showed signs of pregnancy, she set the date for Shiloh's arrival: October 19, 1814. The baby never arrived. Worse, Southcott died just over two months later. But her following did not vanish. In fact, her followers were so avid, they retained her body after her death believing that she would be raised from the dead, and agreed to her burial only after her corpse had begun to decay. Though her following dwindled in the coming years, it continued into the twentieth century in the form of the Panacea Society, a group that believed the Second Coming would take place in Bedford, England—the headquarters of the society. The society owns substantial property in the town, including a house they prepared especially for the Messiah at 18 Albany Street, which they say is the original site of the Garden of Eden. According to their Website, only two members of the society remain alive, and they have nothing to do with the organization's operations. The society continues to exist, however, as a charitable trust, making grants to organizations operating in the Bedford area.

In 1957, a traveling salesman named Mark Prophet founded something called The Summit Lighthouse. The purpose, he said, was to teach the way of the Ascended Masters, people who had achieved so much knowledge and wisdom that they became immortal. After he died in 1973, his wife Elizabeth Clare Prophet renamed the group, calling it the Church Universal and Triumphant. She and her followers moved to a remote Montana ranch patrolled by armed guards. She taught that a coming war with aliens would kill everyone except her and her followers. In the 1980s, the group constructed a mammoth fallout shelter and began stockpiling arms in preparation. The war never materialized, and Elizabeth Clare Prophet died in late 2009. A smaller group of her followers, however, continues to prepare for the end by maintaining a cache of weapons.

In 1997, a group led by a self-proclaimed prophet named Marshall Applewhite believed that the planet Earth was about to be depopulated and that the only chance to survive was to leave as soon as possible. Over the course of three days (from March 24–26, 1997), thirty-nine members of the group committed suicide by ingesting phenobarbital with applesauce or pudding, washing it down with vodka. They prepared by placing a five-dollar bill and three quarters in their pockets, dressing in black shirts, armbands, sweat pants, and new tennis shoes. Then they lay down on their bunks, placed bags over their heads, and waited to leave their bodies and be transported to an alien spaceship they believed was traveling in the wake of the Hale-Bopp Comet.

In the late 1990s, a Taiwanese émigré named Chen Hon Ming began predicting that God would appear on March 25, 1998. About one hundred fifty members of his "God's Salvation Church" gathered in Garland, Texas (which Chen said was chosen because it sounded to him like "God's Land"), where God was expected to appear on Dallas's Channel 18 at 12:01 that morning. It didn't happen. Soon after, Chen and his followers moved to the Buffalo, New York, area, where some—dressed in white smocks and cowboy hats—continued to await the appearance of a "Godplane" that would deliver them from the doom that awaits the rest of the world.

Glocks or Smocks

What would you do—how would you prepare—if you knew the date of the world's end? Would you, like the followers of Joanna Southcott, buy property on or around the site of his expected return?

Would you stockpile weapons against the coming Armageddon, like the Church Universal and Triumphant? Would you pocket $5.75 and swallow poison? Would you dress in a white smock and cowboy hat? Seriously, what would you do?

Many followers of Jesus have answered that question at one time or another. I asked a number of my friends to think about what they would do if they knew the end of the world was just days away.

Sandy Jackson, from Harlem, New York, said, "I would gather with my family to have fun but also to remind them how much they are loved and how proud I am of them."

Joe Bassett of Jacksonville, Florida, said, "I would repair relationships that have been broken. Maybe I would seek to comfort those that are hurting."

"If I'm being honest," said Nashville resident Karen Knickerbocker Pennington, "I'd have my husband and daughter take the week off of school and work so that we can go visiting places that we've never seen. Hopefully I'd be bold enough to share Jesus wherever I go."

And Ashland, Ohio, resident Larry Shade said, "I would make sure as many as possible of my friends and those people who I see every day knew Jesus Christ and accepted him as their Savior."

Those are all good answers. Thoughtful. Insightful. Purposeful. But not one of the people I asked—all followers of Jesus, by the way—gave what may actually be the best answer. None, including myself, referred right away to the action that may be the absolute best way to prepare for the end of the world—whether it comes tomorrow or many years from now. None mentioned the place the Apostle John's vision took him immediately after Jesus' commendations and corrections for his church. None mentioned worship.

Around the Next Corner

It is always interesting to see how our perspectives differ and diverge from God's. It is no different when we read the revelation Jesus gave to his servant John in the last moments of the first century.

After dictating seven messages to the churches in and around John's home church of Ephesus—after systematically telling each church what to continue, what to correct, what to expect in the light of his promised return—Jesus takes John somewhere new.

Before we go there with John, let's stop just for a moment. What would you expect would come next? How would you expect Jesus to follow up his messages to those seven churches? If the purpose of this vision truly was "to show his servants what must soon take place . . . [and to bless] those who hear it and take to heart what is written in it,"[60] what would you think the next words would be? The next sight? The next sound?

Would it be, "After this, the voice said, 'Sell all you have and wait for my return?'"

Would it be, "After this, the voice said, 'Head for the hills. Stockpile weapons. Hunker down.'"

Would it be, "And the voice told me, 'Go, tell your friends and family that time is short?'"

Or, "'Stand on the street corner and preach the Gospel?'"

Or, "'Apologize to your mother?'"

Or, "'Go to confession?'"

Those are some of the things we might consider doing when preparing for the end of the world—right? But those bear virtually no resemblance to Jesus' next priority after issuing praise, correction, and promises to his church in light of the coming apocalypse. Not even close. According to The Revelation, Jesus' next thought was of . . . worship.

John writes:

> After this I looked, and there before me was a door standing open in heaven. And the voice I had first heard speaking to me like a trumpet said, "Come up here, and I will show you what must take place after this." At once I was in the Spirit, and there before me was a throne in heaven

with someone sitting on it. And the one who sat there had the appearance of jasper and carnelian. A rainbow, resembling an emerald, encircled the throne.[61]

John says he was "in the Spirit," just as he said in chapter 1 on the day he received the vision of Christ and the messages to the seven churches. And he again hears a voice like a trumpet (which we know from chapter 1 is Jesus), and he sees a throne in heaven. And his attention, his consciousness, his very heart and nerve and sinew, is focused on one thing: the One who is sitting on the throne.

That, my friend, is worship.

It's not an organ playing. It's not a hymn being sung. It's not an energizing anthem by a choir. It's not a drum solo or a well-preached sermon or a tearjerker of a testimony. It is the focus of the human heart, mind, soul, and strength on the One who is on the throne.

And this vision of John's, in which he reveals to us what heavenly worship—true worship—looks like, shows us that worship is absolutely central to surviving hard times, even to surviving the end of the world. And it shows us that worship is crucial for surviving hard times because of four things that worship—if it is the true worship of the true God—does, four ways the true worship of the true and living God will get you ready for the end of the world when it comes.

Get Reoriented

One of the casualties of our modern ways and cool technology in public worship these days is context. I often read Scripture on my phone or from a large projection screen in public worship services. And there are advantages to doing so. For example, on my phone (or iPad), I can quickly jump to a cross-reference. I can easily highlight text or type in a note. I can look up definitions or resources.

But there are disadvantages, too. When I'm reading the text on a screen, I have almost no sense of the context. I may remember—or be told—what precedes or follows the portion I am reading, but it's just not the same as when I have an actual hard-copy Bible open in my hands. Then, at a glance, I can see a much broader context for what I'm reading.

The same is true when you're reading a book like this one. The author or book designer cannot show you the whole sweep and scope of the passage being cited. So, for that reason, let me recommend that you actually take a minute to open your Bible, alongside this book, to the fourth and fifth chapters of The Revelation. I'd like you to notice that the position of everything in those two chapters is described *as it relates to the throne.*

Look at verse 3. It says:

A rainbow, resembling an emerald, **encircled the throne.**[62]

Then verse 4 begins:

Surrounding the throne were twenty-four other thrones.[63]

Verse 5 says:

From the throne came flashes of lightning, rumblings and peals of thunder.[64]

The latter part of verse 5:

Before the throne, seven lamps were blazing.[65]

And verse 6:

> Also **before the throne** there was what looked like a sea
> of glass, clear as crystal.[66]

And again in verse 6:

> In the center, **around the throne**, were four living crea-
> tures.[67]

Verse 10:

> The twenty-four elders fall down **before him who sits on
> the throne**, and worship him who lives for ever and ever.
> They lay their crowns **before the throne**.[68]

And it keeps going. In chapter 5, verse 6, it says,

> Then I saw a Lamb, looking as if it had been slain, stand-
> ing **in the center of the throne**.[69]

And in chapter 5, verse 11:

> Then I looked and heard the voice of many angels, num-
> bering thousands upon thousands, and ten thousand
> times ten thousand. They **encircled the throne**.[70]

Everything in this scene from John's vision is described by its position in relation to the throne of God.

That is what worship does. Not only in heaven, but on earth. Not
only for the angels, but for me. And for you.

It orients me, and everything around me, in relation to the throne
of God. In worship, I focus on God. Not on me, not on my ideas,

not on my preferences, my comfort, my desires. But on the One who sits on the throne.

This is where we go so wrong in what we call worship these days. We come to "worship" with our agenda. We put ourselves—our priorities, our comforts, our likes and dislikes—on the throne:

> "Oh, don't play that song, I don't like that one."
> "Oh, good, they're gonna sing my favorite song now."
> "Oh, no, is he preaching again?"
> "Why is her hair like that?"
> "Why is it so loud?"
> "Why is it so warm?"
> "Why is it so cold?"

Can you imagine John, being caught up "in the Spirit," seeing a throne in heaven and One who sat on it who had a dazzling appearance, while thunder rumbles and lightning flashes from the throne, and voices angelic and human all cry out, "Holy, holy, holy," and John sees and hears all this—can you imagine him saying, "I'd like it better if the thunder wasn't so loud and the lightning wasn't so bright"?

Can you imagine him saying, "Look at what those angels are wearing. Is that really appropriate?"

No, of course, you can't imagine that, because you know and I know that the true worship of the true God is focused on God, oriented around God, and intent on what *he* gets out of it, not what *I* get out of it. It reminds me who is on the throne. It points my heart and my life toward him. It focuses me on who is important and, in light of that fact, on what is important.

Worship reorients. It must, or it is not worship. And if we are not giving that kind of worship, we are not prepared for the apocalypse.

Get Reconciled

John's vision of heavenly worship not only reveals the reorienting influence of true worship, it shows us something else, something wonderful. Look at Revelation 4:4–8, which says,

> Surrounding the throne were twenty-four other thrones, and seated on them were twenty-four elders. They were dressed in white and had crowns of gold on their heads. From the throne came flashes of lightning, rumblings and peals of thunder. Before the throne, seven lamps were blazing. These are the seven spirits of God. Also before the throne there was what looked like a sea of glass, clear as crystal.
>
> In the center, around the throne, were four living creatures, and they were covered with eyes, in front and in back. The first living creature was like a lion, the second was like an ox, the third had a face like a man, the fourth was like a flying eagle. Each of the four living creatures had six wings and was covered with eyes all around, even under his wings. Day and night they never stop saying:

> "Holy, holy, holy
> is the Lord God Almighty,
> who was, and is, and is to come."[71]

John describes twenty-four thrones, and twenty-four "elders" on them. There's more than a little scholarly debate about those thrones and those elders, but, long story short, most agree that the twenty-four thrones unite the twelve patriarchs, representing the twelve tribes of Israel, and the twelve disciples, representing the New Israel, the church.

He also describes four living creatures, freaky winged eye-covered beings that the Old Testament prophet Ezekiel also described—
one like a lion,
one like an ox,

one like a man,
and one like an eagle,[72]
the symbolism of which is very deep and broad, with parallels to the life
and ministry of Jesus and his depiction in the four Gospels, and more.
And then, way down in verse 11 of Revelation 5, he describes
another group of beings:

> Then I looked and heard the voice of many angels, num-
> bering thousands upon thousands, and ten thousand
> times ten thousand. They encircled the throne and the
> living creatures and the elders.[73]

Now, don't miss this—this is big. In these verses, we see
Hebrew patriarchs and Christian apostles,
humans and angels,
the mineral kingdom and animal kingdom,
wild animals and domesticated livestock,
rainbows of color and blazing white,
all uniting around the throne of God, all reconciled at the throne of
God.
Because worship reconciles. Worship unites. Worship harmonizes.
That is why,

> Whenever the living creatures give glory, honor and thanks
> to him who sits on the throne and who lives for ever and
> ever, the twenty-four elders fall down before him who sits
> on the throne and worship him who lives for ever and ever.
> They lay their crowns before the throne and say:
> "You are worthy, our Lord and God,
> to receive glory and honor and power,
> for you created all things,
> and by your will they were created
> and have their being."[74]

Worship reconciles . . . if it is the true worship of the true God. That's why, if you are trying to worship God and you are unreconciled with a brother or sister, Jesus says,

> If you are offering your gift at the altar and there remember that your brother has something against you, leave your gift there in front of the altar. First go and be reconciled to your brother; then come and offer your gift.[75]

If you are trying to worship and are still holding a grudge, refusing to forgive, hating someone in your heart, you are totally sabotaging your worship. You are on a fool's errand. You may be singing better than anyone, you may be clapping, jumping, kneeling—you may even be taking notes while the preacher preaches—but, whatever else you are doing, you are not truly worshiping the one true God, because that kind of worship reconciles. And, because it reconciles, it also prepares you for the end of the world, in a way that nothing else will.

Get Revelation

Look at the beginning of Revelation 5:

> Then I saw in the right hand of him who sat on the throne a scroll with writing on both sides and sealed with seven seals. And I saw a mighty angel proclaiming in a loud voice, "Who is worthy to break the seals and open the scroll?" But no one in heaven or on earth or under the earth could open the scroll or even look inside it. I wept and wept because no one was found who was worthy to open the scroll or look inside. Then one of the elders said to me, "Do not weep! See, the Lion of the tribe of Judah, the Root of David, has triumphed. He is able to open the scroll and its seven seals."

Then I saw a Lamb, looking as if it had been slain, standing in the center of the throne, encircled by the four living creatures and the elders. He had seven horns and seven eyes, which are the seven spirits of God sent out into all the earth. He came and took the scroll from the right hand of him who sat on the throne. And when he had taken it, the four living creatures and the twenty-four elders fell down before the Lamb. Each one had a harp and they were holding golden bowls full of incense, which are the prayers of the saints. And they sang a new song:

> "You are worthy to take the scroll
>> and to open its seals,
> because you were slain,
>> and with your blood you purchased men for God
> from every tribe and language and people and nation.

> You have made them to be a kingdom and priests to serve our God,
>> and they will reign on the earth."[76]

In the midst of his worship, John sees a scroll in the hand of God, the One who sits on the throne, sealed with seven seals. But at first there is no one in heaven or earth or under the earth—that is, no created being—who has the authority to break the seals and open the scroll. These seals he describes are not padlocks; they are wax seals, which some crafty people still use today to seal envelopes.

It wasn't a question of no one having the physical ability to break the seal; it was the authority, the right to open it, that was unclaimed. If you bring to me a manila envelope that says, "CIA, TOP SECRET: FOR THE DIRECTOR'S EYES ONLY," I'm not going to open it. I may have the physical ability to tear it open—

with my bare hands, even. But I know I don't have the clearance. I lack the authority. And I don't want to end up in some secret prison somewhere.

So it was here. No one could open the scroll—which a first-century Christian would have clearly recognized as Scripture—until Jesus showed up.

And so it is today.

The scroll—the Word of God—must be central to our worship. The fact that the scroll of Revelation 5 has seven seals indicates a complete revelation, perfect and priceless, because seven is the number of perfection in the Bible.

If the scroll, the Scripture, is not becoming more and more to you—more and more precious, more and more real, more and more life changing—then whatever else you're doing, you're not worshiping, because worship reveals and enlightens the Word of God.

But—and this is crucial—we risk great harm to ourselves if we open the scroll ourselves. We make a grave mistake if we study the Bible without waiting on Jesus to reveal himself in his Word, without submitting to him and listening for his voice in it.

If you accustom yourself to hearing and reading and studying the Bible without inviting and involving the Word himself[77] into the process, then you risk hardening your heart against the very words you are reading. So much error results, in doctrine and in life, when we are "self-taught" in the Word, rather than Spirit-taught, because revelation of the Word by the Word is crucial to true worship, and it is crucial to surviving the end of the world.

Get Revived

Revelation 5, beginning at verse 11, says:

> Then I looked and heard the voice of many angels, numbering thousands upon thousands, and ten thousand

times ten thousand. They encircled the throne and the
living creatures and the elders. In a loud voice they sang:

"Worthy is the Lamb, who was slain,
   to receive power and wealth and wisdom and strength
   and honor and glory and praise!"

Then I heard every creature in heaven and on earth and under the earth and on the sea, and all that is in them, singing:
   "To him who sits on the throne and to the Lamb
   be praise and honor and glory and power,
      for ever and ever!"

The four living creatures said, "Amen," and the elders fell
down and worshiped.[78]

You have already noticed that everything is oriented around the
throne, everyone is singing to the One on the throne, everyone is
united, rejoicing, focused on the worthiness of God. Can you imagine the majesty and sheer volume of ten thousand times ten thousand angels singing in a loud voice?

Do you know how loud an angel can sing? I don't, either, but I
bet it's pretty loud. And notice what they sing:

Worthy is the Lamb, who was slain,
   to receive power and wealth and wisdom and strength
   and honor and glory and praise![79]

Power, wealth, wisdom, strength, honor, glory, and praise.

There's the number seven again, meaning the One on the throne
is perfectly and completely worthy.

And the song is so infectious that every creature in heaven and on
earth and under the earth gets in on the party, singing,

To him who sits on the throne and to the Lamb
be praise and honor and glory and power,
for ever and ever![80]

In my decades of ministry as a pastor, there have been many times when I have entered a prayer meeting or a worship celebration feeling tired or discouraged. Even depressed. Ministry can be brutal. *Life* can be brutal. But I honestly can never remember an occasion when I have truly worshiped and left the same way I entered. Because worship revives. Worship restores. It screws my head on straight and recharges my heart and reorients my life and refocuses me on what matters . . . and *who* matters.

It will do the same for you. It will bring heaven to earth. It will bring heaven to *you*. And it will prepare you—perhaps more than anything else—for "what must soon take place."[81]

Prayer

Father God, lead me back to the heart of worship. Let my daily worship and my weekly worship with others reorient me and place me in the right posture in relation to your throne, in relation to your rule over all. Make my worship pleasing to you; make it also an impetus for repentance and reconciliation with others.

Holy Spirit, teach me as I read.and study your Word. Lead me into all truth, as Jesus promised.

And, Lord Jesus, you who are worthy to receive power and wealth and wisdom and strength and honor and glory and praise, revive and restore me through the worship I offer. Let my worship bring joy to you. Let it bring heaven to me. Amen.

5

Can't Touch This

Tell me what's John writin'? Ask the Revelator.
What's John writin'? Ask the Revelator.
What's John writin'? Ask the Revelator:
A book of the seven seals
                                                —Blind Willie Johnson

At 9:45 A.M. on Monday, October 15, 2001—less than five weeks after the momentous 9/11 terrorist attacks in the United States—Grant Leslie, an aide to Senate Majority Leader Tom Daschle, opened an envelope hand-addressed to the senator. The contents of the envelope: death.

That envelope contained two grams of white powder, composed of billions of spores of anthrax, a deadly substance. It was one of seven letters, authorities learned later, that had been mailed to news media offices and two U.S. senators over the course of four weeks. Five people died from touching or inhaling the spores; seventeen others were infected. The attacks, coming in the wake of the devastating 9/11 attacks, spread fear and suspicion for months to come.

The Revelation of Jesus Christ to the Apostle John presents an eerily similar picture after the uplifting heavenly worship described in chapters 4 and 5. But, like the rest of the vision given to John, its purpose is not to engender fear and suspicion, but blessing and hope.

Four Horsemen

Many people consider chapters 6 and 7 of The Revelation some of the most frightening pages in Scripture. They tell of four horsemen who ride forth to wreak destruction and misery on the earth. They depict the souls of martyrs who were slain for their devotion to God. They portray a great earthquake and the sun going dark and the moon turning blood red and the stars falling to earth. They show even the most powerful people on earth fleeing to the hills and begging for death.

In the twenty centuries since this vision was first revealed and published, many thoughtful people have interpreted them in many different ways. Nicolas of Lyra, in the fourteenth century, saw the events of the first century in the seals of Revelation 6 and later events in the seven trumpets and seven bowls. Other commentators believe that the seals present a grand sweep of the redemption story from Jesus' ascension to his second coming, while the trumpets and bowls that follow in Revelation 8–9 and 15–16 supply more details on those same events.[82] Still others view the seals, trumpets, and bowls together as cyclical, describing a pattern that is seen over and over throughout history.[83] And Tim Lahaye, who has sold more end times–related books than anyone in history, sees the seals, trumpets, and bowls as sequential horrors taking place in the tribulation period between the rapture of the saints and the Second Coming of Jesus.[84]

They can't all be right, of course. And regardless of which of those views (if any) is correct, the bleak picture painted by the seven seals does seem at first glance to call into doubt the stated purpose of Jesus in giving us The Revelation: "to show his servants what must soon take place . . . [and to bless] those who hear it and take to heart what is written in it."[85] Are we really supposed to feel blessed by the prospect of death and destruction? Are we supposed to take heart and find hope in a vision of martyrdom? Can anyone seriously believe that the sun going dark and the moon turning red are inducements to hope?

The short answer is: yes.

Because the events of Revelation 6 and 7 are a pointed message to the faithful followers and worshipers of Jesus. Remember, the first five chapters of The Revelation tell us that we should feel blessed, that we should focus on Jesus and feel his touch. They have brought praise, correction, and promise to the receptive heart. They have prepared us for the end of all things via the reorienting, reconciling, revealing, and reviving power of worship. If those things are happening in us, then perhaps we are primed for a new perspective on the things happening around us, which forms the basis of the next part of this amazing revelation.

Revelation 6 and 7 can engender courage and hope if they are seen as two sides of a coin, or perhaps more as a voice and an echo. Chapter 6 paints a brutally honest picture of the conditions that surround us as followers of Jesus, and chapter 7 depicts our relationship to those conditions.

Recognize the Evil That Surrounds You

Chapter 5 of The Revelation describes the scroll with seven seals, and the only one in all of heaven and earth who is worthy to break the seals and unroll the scrolls—the Lamb of God, whose praises heaven sings. Chapter 6 begins with these words:

I watched as the Lamb opened the first of the seven seals.[86]

The opening of that first seal was like the opening of the anthrax letter in Senator Daschle's office: it released something terrible, and each successive seal let loose a malignant force on the earth. Each of these seals represents a very real and very present evil abroad in the world, which even the most casual observer must admit and which the sincere follower of Jesus Christ must lament:

Tyranny

Then I heard one of the four living creatures say in a voice like thunder, "Come!" I looked, and there before me was a white horse! Its rider held a bow, and he was given a crown, and he rode out as a conqueror bent on conquest.[87]

Each of the four living creatures—the angelic sentinels that surround the throne, described in chapter 4—calls forth a horse and rider representing an evil that has existed since the entrance of sin into the world but which will be felt with increasing fury as the end of the world approaches.

The first of these ominous horsemen rides a white horse, a symbol of military power. In his hand is another military emblem, the archer's bow. On his head is a crown, signifying governmental authority.

Embedded in this image may be a reference to Rome's most troublesome enemies. A little over a hundred years before The Revelation was written, in 53 BC, a man named Marcus Crassus, the third member of Rome's ruling Triumvirate (with Julius Caesar and Pompey), decided to launch a Roman invasion of the Parthian Empire (in what is today's Iraq and Iran). His army of nearly forty thousand infantry and four thousand cavalry crossed the Euphrates to confront a Parthian army of about nine thousand mounted archers and one thousand heavy cavalry.

In the desolate territory around the city of Carrhae (today's Harran, near the border of Turkey and Syria), the Roman legions were quickly surrounded by the Parthian horsemen and the deadly rain of arrows shot from their distinctive and powerful bows. When Crassus ordered a retreat, the Parthians swept in and massacred the four thousand wounded soldiers he left behind. The next day, the Parthian general Surena offered a truce that would allow the Roman army to withdraw safely to Syria. The unnerved Crassus was reluctant, but his troops threatened mutiny. At the meeting, a Parthian pulled at the reins of Crassus's horse, and a melee ensued. Crassus and his generals were murdered, and the rest of the Roman army was captured or killed.

Rome's defeat at the hands of the Parthians was more than costly. It was humiliating. For generations, Rome's armies had seemed invincible. They had rolled over every foe and conquered every country they encountered. But the disaster at Carrhae shattered that aura of invincibility and halted the eastward march of the Roman Empire.

The shock of that event may have rippled through the Roman Empire much as the September 11 terrorist attacks on the United States—and their aftermath—rumbled through the post 9/11 world. The depiction of tyranny as a crowned archer on a white horse may have evoked more terror than we can imagine to a group of Christians in the eastern part of the Roman Empire.

In our day, no less than in John's, we are familiar with tyranny, from Syria to Egypt, from North Korea to Cuba. We read of protestors being shot and pastors being imprisoned. We hear of rulers living in unimaginable splendor while their citizens struggle in incomprehensible squalor. The rider on the white horse still rides today and will torment the inhabitants of the earth and the followers of Christ while time speeds forward to the end of the world.

War

When the Lamb opened the second seal, I heard the second living creature say, "Come!" Then another horse came out, a fiery red one. Its rider was given power to take peace from the earth and to make people kill each other. To him was given a large sword.[88]

The second seal releases the red horse, the color of blood. Many scholars and students have noted the correspondence between these six seals and Jesus' description of the end as recorded in Matthew 24:

"Watch out that no one deceives you. For many will come in my name, claiming, 'I am the Messiah,' and will deceive many. You will hear of wars and rumors of wars, but see to it that you are not alarmed. Such things must happen, but the end is still to come. Nation will rise against nation, and kingdom against kingdom. There will be famines and earthquakes in various places. All these are the beginning of birth pains.

"Then you will be handed over to be persecuted and put to death, and you will be hated by all nations because of me.

At that time many will turn away from the faith and will betray and hate each other, and many false prophets will appear and deceive many people. Because of the increase of wickedness, the love of most will grow cold, but the one who stands firm to the end will be saved."[89]

The second horseman of the apocalypse is the harbinger of "wars and rumors of wars." In the short space of the twentieth century alone, 160 million people died—which some estimate as roughly the world population at the time The Revelation was recorded. And the second horseman shows no sign of slowing down, from U.S. action in Afghanistan and Iraq to civil war in Ivory Coast, tribal conflict in Ituri, uprisings in Libya and Bahrain, unrest in Chechnya, and genocide in Sudan.

But remember, Jesus said, "You will hear of wars and rumors of wars, but see to it that you are not alarmed. Such things must happen, but the end is still to come."[90] How often have we—and those who have gone before us—thoroughly ignored Jesus' words? How many times have we responded to "wars and rumors of wars" with alarm? Obviously, concern—even dismay—is natural anytime the red horse rides. But Jesus' words ought to remind us of two things: (1) he is still sovereign, and (2) our task is not to panic or guess or calculate the time of his return but to stand firm to the end.

Famine

When the Lamb opened the third seal, I heard the third living creature say, "Come!" I looked, and there before me was a black horse! Its rider was holding a pair of scales in his hand. Then I heard what sounded like a voice among the four living creatures, saying, "Two pounds of wheat for a day's wages, and six pounds of barley for a day's wages, and do not damage the oil and the wine!"[91]

The third horse depicts scarcity and shortage, deprivation and depression. As Jesus warned, "There will be famines."[92] The voice John describes, announcing "Two pounds of wheat for a day's wages, and six pounds of barley for a day's wages," portrays subsistence living, a situation where necessities cost so much there would be no chance of saving or getting ahead. At the same time, however, oil and wine—niceties enjoyed by the wealthy—would be unaffected. It describes the rich doing just fine while shortages and rising prices squeeze the life out of everyone else. Thus, the rider on the black horse symbolizes not only scarcity and deprivation but economic injustice, too.

This third seal says that economic disparity and daily hardship should not shock or overwhelm us. This does not mean we should not work to correct such problems and ease their effects. It reminds us, however, that they are certainties, not surprises, as the end approaches.

Disease

> When the Lamb opened the fourth seal, I heard the voice of the fourth living creature say, "Come!" I looked, and there before me was a pale horse! Its rider was named Death, and Hades was following close behind him. They were given power over a fourth of the earth to kill by sword, famine and plague, and by the wild beasts of the earth.[93]

The fourth horseman is the specter of disease. Despite all the advances of science and medicine in the past twenty centuries, the world continues to be plagued by the rider on the pale horse ("sickly green" in the J. B. Phillips version).[94] HIV (human immunodeficiency virus) afflicts nearly forty million people worldwide, leading many to die of various complications, including AIDS. Pneumonia and other respiratory diseases claim four million lives a year. More than a million people each year die of malaria, two million from tuberculosis, and another two million from meningitis. Outbreaks of

SARS (Severe Acute Respiratory Syndrome), swine flu, and avian flu continue to be a concern of health organizations.

This is not only life in a fallen world; it is also life in a world speeding toward apocalypse. Utopian fantasies of the eradication of all disease are just that—fantasies. I write as the grandfather of two beautiful children with cystic fibrosis, a genetic disease that causes thick, sticky mucus to build up in the lungs, digestive tract, and other areas of the body, resulting in life-threatening lung infections and serious digestion problems. Like many others, I will do all I can on this earth to find a cure for that disease. But I also know that my ultimate hope—and theirs—is not in this world, where the pale horse still rides forth, for here on this earth and in this life the second, third, and fourth riders together have been given "power over a fourth of the earth to kill by sword, famine and plague, and by the wild beasts of the earth," as verse 8 says.

Oppression

> When he opened the fifth seal, I saw under the altar the souls of those who had been slain because of the word of God and the testimony they had maintained. They called out in a loud voice, "How long, Sovereign Lord, holy and true, until you judge the inhabitants of the earth and avenge our blood?" Then each of them was given a white robe, and they were told to wait a little longer, until the full number of their fellow servants, their brothers and sisters, were killed just as they had been.[95]

Most followers of Jesus in the Western world tend to think of martyrs as people of the past and future, not the present. You know, Stephen and James, Thomas Beckett and John Huss, and so on. However, our brothers and sisters in places such as China, Pakistan, Afghanistan, Syria, Iran, and North Korea think differently. To many Christ-followers in the twenty-first century, martyrdom is a clear and present danger.

Ri Hyon Ok was a thirty-three-year-old mother of three who was publicly executed by the North Korean government on June 16, 2009, for the crime of giving away Bibles. Her husband and children were banished to North Korea's vast political prison system the day after she was killed.

Eight Egyptian Christians (Copts) were massacred by Muslim gunmen as they left Christmas services in the city of Nag Hammadi on January 7, 2010 (the date of Christmas according to the Coptic calendar). In addition to the eight Copts, a Muslim bystander was also killed. Nine Copts and two Muslims were wounded. Two other Coptic Christian women were killed in nearby villages when angry mobs set their homes on fire. Businesses owned by Christians were also looted and destroyed in the accompanying attacks. Thirteen months later, an Egyptian court acquitted two of the three suspects; the third, who unintentionally killed the single Muslim victim, was sentenced to death.

Minorities Minister Shahbaz Bhatti, the only Christian in the Pakistani cabinet, was killed March 2, 2011, when gunmen ambushed his vehicle outside his home. Bhatti had promised to change Pakistan's draconian blasphemy laws targeting Christians and other minorities. He had continued his efforts even after a powerful ally in that cause had been murdered two months earlier.

Ugandan pastor Alufunzi Ziwa was reportedly beaten and killed by the enemies of the Gospel on his way home from a class at Faith Bible College–Lugazi on August 12, 2011. In addition to being a pastor, father, and husband, Ziwa was the director of a village school and a local medical care provider.

We may be assured that each of these souls is among the many who are crying out, "How long, Sovereign Lord, holy and true, until you judge the inhabitants of the earth and avenge our blood?" But notice that the fifth seal reveals the martyrs in heaven crying out, not their survivors on the earth. The martyrs' suffering is ended. Their struggle is over. They are robed in white. We might not be surprised to see them resting in the arms of God. We might expect them to be celebrating their deliverance from suffering. But they are not. Why not? We are not told, but it may be that they cry out not for their sake but for the sake of justice and, perhaps, for the sake of their living brothers and sisters.

The Lord, however, does not answer their "how long" question. He tells them to wait until the ranks of those to be martyred in Jesus' name—whom God in his foreknowledge already knows—are filled. Someday, someone will be the last name added to the martyrs' roll, and none but God knows for whom that honor is reserved. In other words, while oppression surrounds us and even afflicts us, it can also honor us, if we are chosen to suffer for the Name.[96]

Disaster

I watched as he opened the sixth seal. There was a great earthquake. The sun turned black like sackcloth made of goat hair, the whole moon turned blood red, and the stars in the sky fell to earth, as figs drop from a fig tree when shaken by a strong wind. The heavens receded like a scroll being rolled up, and every mountain and island was removed from its place.

Then the kings of the earth, the princes, the generals, the rich, the mighty, and everyone else, both slave and free, hid in caves and among the rocks of the mountains. They called to the mountains and the rocks, "Fall on us and hide us from the face of him who sits on the throne and from the wrath of the Lamb! For the great day of their wrath has come, and who can withstand it?"[97]

The opening of the sixth seal visits on the earth a global cataclysm of truly apocalyptic proportions. Earthquake. Eclipse. Meteors. Natural disasters that will produce terror and panic such as the world has never before seen.

Three things are clear from the revelation of the sixth seal in John's vision. First, the disaster he describes is universal in its scope. In other words, it isn't a localized disaster like the massive earthquake and tsunami that devastated Japan in 2011. It is global in scale. Second, as John describes it, the disasters that follow the opening of the sixth seal are unavoidable. That is, unlike the economic calamity associated with the third seal, in which the luxuries enjoyed primarily by the rich are untouched, *no one* will be sheltered or unaffected by these disasters. Kings, princes, generals, the rich, the mighty, both slave and free, are utterly traumatized.

Third, the sixth seal unleashes a disaster that is unmistakable in its source. The Revelation shows rich, poor, mighty, and weak all calling out for protection from "the face of him who sits on the throne and from the wrath of the Lamb!"[98] The people who are affected apparently do not debate whether these events are the wrath of God or not. They do not question the source of these events. They are depicted as being uniformly aware that "the great day of [God's] wrath"[99] is upon them.

None of us is exempt from the forces of nature. Floods and earthquakes, tornadoes and tsunamis do not play favorites, and their effects not only destroy property but also break hearts. Disasters will come and go as long as this age endures, as will tyranny, war, famine, death, and oppression. Those things surround us. But they need not rule us.

Realize That Evil Need Not Confound You

Revelation 6 is not likely to be chosen as the most encouraging chapter in the Bible. You won't find its seventeen verses in many greeting cards. It's probably not going to inspire a new Hillsong or Jesus Culture worship album. But it does fit in with The Revelation's stated purpose "to show his servants what must soon take place . . . [and to bless] those who hear it and take to heart what is written in it."[100]

The distress, disease, and disasters of chapter 6 are a necessary prelude to the message of chapter 7. As I said earlier in this

chapter, Revelation 6 and 7 can be profitably approached and
understood as a voice and an echo. Because the picture painted
in Revelation 6 is so disturbing, the vision presented in chapter
7 is all the more important. Though chapter 6 may dismay us,
chapter 7 ought to delight us, with its message of hope and its
promise of blessing. In fact, I've written two verses in the margin
of my Bible, one at the beginning of chapter 6 and the other at
the end of chapter 7. They are like bookends to my understanding
of these passages. The first is from 1 John and the second is from
Psalm 91:

> We know that anyone born of God does not continue to
> sin; the One who was born of God keeps them safe, and
> the evil one cannot harm them.[101]

> A thousand may fall at your side,
> ten thousand at your right hand,
> but it will not come near you.[102]

Those verses seem odd—impossible, even—in the light of Revelation 6. How can they be true, when God's Word promises so much
calamity? That is why we must not stop reading but must continue to
chapter 7. It reveals seven things that are true of anyone born of God.
Seven things that are true of me and, I pray, of you. Seven things
from which we must take comfort and courage.

You Are Sealed

After this I saw four angels standing at the four corners
of the earth, holding back the four winds of the earth to
prevent any wind from blowing on the land or on the sea
or on any tree. Then I saw another angel coming up from
the east, having the seal of the living God. He called out in
a loud voice to the four angels who had been given power

to harm the land and the sea: "Do not harm the land or the sea or the trees until we put a seal on the foreheads of the servants of our God." Then I heard the number of those who were sealed: 144,000 from all the tribes of Israel.

From the tribe of Judah 12,000 were sealed,
from the tribe of Reuben 12,000,
from the tribe of Gad 12,000,
from the tribe of Asher 12,000,
from the tribe of Naphtali 12,000,
from the tribe of Manasseh 12,000,
from the tribe of Simeon 12,000,
from the tribe of Levi 12,000,
from the tribe of Issachar 12,000,
from the tribe of Zebulun 12,000,
from the tribe of Joseph 12,000,
from the tribe of Benjamin 12,000.[103]

As the seventh chapter of The Revelation begins, it is as if a giant cosmic "pause" button is pressed. The sixth seal has been broken, but the seventh seal is not yet opened when John sees four angels at the four corners of the earth, holding back the four winds. In other words, everything stops. All is suspended. No one moves. A fifth angel comes on the scene, holding a signet ring representing the absolute authority of the Living God and announces that no harm can come to the earth until the servants of God are sealed.

Both the sealing and the number of those sealed are rich with symbolism. To be sealed means to belong to God and to be under his sovereign, almighty protection. This "seal" corresponds to the "mark" mentioned in Ezekiel's prophecy:

> The LORD called to the man clothed in linen who had the writing kit at his side and said to him, "Go throughout

the city of Jerusalem and put a mark on the foreheads of those who grieve and lament over all the detestable things that are done in it."[104]

The word translated "mark" in Ezekiel's prophecy is the Hebrew Tau, the name of the last letter of the Hebrew alphabet, which was shaped like a cross. It is the symbol of the One who is born of God[105] and belongs to God. It is the shadow of the cross, which seals our salvation and places us under God's protection.

The number of those sealed is also symbolic. To a first-century Christ-follower, it would have been an almost inconceivably high number and a thoroughly complete one. It is the multiple of the number twelve squared and the number ten squared. The number twelve reflects both the tribes of Israel and the twelve apostles, representing the church. Multiplied again by 10^2, the total of 144,000 signifies absolute completeness—those from every age, every tribe, every corner of the world.

And you—you are among that number. You are sealed. You are counted among those who belong to God. You are under God's protection. Not one is excluded. Not one is forgotten. You are sealed and safe from anything and everything—now and forever—that does not meet with God's approval.

You Are Connected

After this I looked, and there before me was a great multitude that no one could count, from every nation, tribe, people and language, standing before the throne and before the Lamb.[106]

John's next comment reinforces the symbolism of the numbering and listing of the 144,000. Notice that in verse 4, he says, "I heard the number of those who were sealed." He didn't see that there were 144,000; he heard the number of them. After hearing that there were twelve thousand from twelve different tribes, he says, "I looked, and there before me was a great multitude that no one could count." In other words, he heard the symbolic number, but he saw a multitude so great they could not be counted. This is not contradictory; it is simply a shift from the auditory to the visual.

He also perceives what was represented by the multiple of the number twelve squared and the number ten squared—that is, that this great multitude includes people from every nation and tribe, all people groups and language groups. It is the fulfillment of the promise and potential contained in the Day of Pentecost, when in Jerusalem John experienced "Parthians, Medes and Elamites; residents of Mesopotamia, Judea and Cappadocia, Pontus and Asia, Phrygia and Pamphylia, Egypt and the parts of Libya near Cyrene; visitors from Rome (both Jews and converts to Judaism); Cretans and Arabs,"[107] all discovering the grace of God.

And you are there in that picture, too. You are connected to that vast, innumerable multitude. You are not subject to the conflict and bigotry, the hatred and division that characterize the forces of Revelation 6. You belong to the multitude of Revelation 7, if you are indeed sealed by the cross and are indeed "born of God."[108] You are connected to the Norwegian and Egyptian, to black and white, to Asian and Latino, to speakers of Arabic and those with strange accents. You and I. You and all. Connected. Belonging. At home before the throne and before the Lamb.

You Are Pure

They were wearing white robes.[109]

The promise of Jesus to some of his faithful followers in the church at Sardis was that "They will walk with me, dressed in white, for they are worthy."[110] John's subsequent vision of the great multitude in Revelation 7 depicts the fulfillment of that promise to those souls and to many, many others. John not only sees but mentions that the vast multitude was wearing white robes.

The white robes of the multitude signify their purity. William Pearson, an early member of The Salvation Army, wrote a song with these words as the chorus:

> In white, in white, walking in white.
> He makes me worthy through His blood
> To walk with Him in white.[111]

From our earthbound point of view, we tend to rank ourselves and those around us according to fallible and changeable perceptions of righteousness. We know how often we stumble. We know how messy our lives are at times. And we tend to rank others as either better or worse than us, based on what we see of their lives, compared to what we know of ours.

Though evil may surround you, it need not confound you. Though a thousand may fall at your side, it will not come near you. If you are marked by the cross, you have been made worthy through his blood to walk with him in white.

You Are Victorious

They . . . were holding palm branches in their hands.[112]

In 164 BC, a man named Judas Maccabeus led a band of Jewish freedom fighters to victory over the Syrian armies that had occupied Jerusalem and oppressed the Jews since the time of Alexander the Great. The crowds celebrated this great victory by waving palm branches as they entered the temple courts on the occasion of its rededication (an event still celebrated annually in the feast of Hanukkah). Jewish coins of that period were stamped with palm branches to remind everyone of this great victory (in fact, when Roman coins bearing the image of Tiberius Caesar appeared in the Galilee in the first century AD, some local Jews stamped palm branches across the emperor's face as an act of defiance).

Roughly two hundred years after Judas Maccabeus's victory, Jesus of Nazareth appeared outside Jerusalem, riding a donkey into the holy city. Many in the crowd, recognizing the messianic significance of the moment, ran out to greet him, waving palm branches and shouting, "Hosanna" (which means, "Save us!"). It was a cry, not for spiritual help, but for military victory.

So, when John recognizes palm branches in the hands of the great multitude in white robes, it means these people are not bedraggled. They are not wounded or weary. They are unbowed. They are "more than conquerors."[113] They are victorious.

And you are among them. Not only at some future time, but now. Your victory is not only a possibility; it is a reality. Whether the world ends today or after your lifetime matters little. You are victorious, not through your efforts, but by the work and will of Jesus Christ.

As Eugene Peterson writes,

> The Revelation summarizes the context: admit evil and do not fear it—for "he who is in you is greater than he who is in the world" (1 John 4:4); endure evil, for you are already triumphant over it—"I saw Satan fall like lightning from heaven" (Luke 10:18).[114]

You Are God's Servant

And they cried out in a loud voice:

> "Salvation belongs to our God,
> who sits on the throne,
> and to the Lamb."

All the angels were standing around the throne and around the elders and the four living creatures. They fell down on their faces before the throne and worshiped God, saying:

"Amen!
Praise and glory
and wisdom and thanks and honor
and power and strength
be to our God for ever and ever.
Amen!"

Then one of the elders asked me, "These in white robes—
who are they, and where did they come from?"
    I answered, "Sir, you know."
    And he said, "These are they who have come out of
the great tribulation; they have washed their robes and
made them white in the blood of the Lamb. Therefore,
    "they are before the throne of God
            and serve him day and night in his temple;
    and he who sits on the throne
            will shelter them with his presence.
    'Never again will they hunger;
            never again will they thirst.
    The sun will not beat down on them,'
            nor any scorching heat.
    For the Lamb at the center of the throne
            will be their shepherd;
    'he will lead them to springs of living water.'
            'And God will wipe away every tear from their
eyes.'"[115]

Do you see yourself in that multitude? As one of those esteemed servants of God? As one who has—or will—come through great tribulation and yet is robed in white? That is the vision Jesus gave to John
. . . about *you*. And, yes, it is about all who are redeemed by the Lamb
and sealed in him. But it is also about you. Specifically, you. You are

among that multitude. It is more real and more present than the socks you are wearing or the thoughts you are thinking.

You Are Sheltered in His Tent

Another truth about you in that passage from Revelation 7 is easy to miss and more so depending on the Bible translation you may be reading. But it is both beautiful and important. The words of the elder before God's throne (I like to think that it was Peter, the most verbal of the twelve, but the text doesn't specify, of course) promise that "he who sits on the throne will shelter them with his presence."[116] Other translations say,

> The one who sits on the throne will spread his tent over them (GWT, CEV).

> He who sits on the throne will spread His tabernacle over them (NASB).

> He who is seated on the throne shall overshadow them with his care (Moffatt[117]).

While evil surrounds you, it should not confound you, because you are safe in God's tent. He has spread his tabernacle over you. He overshadows you with his care. Those are the facts, the realities, of your life now . . . and forever.

My mother, who died of breast cancer when I was still a boy, was a gifted and classically trained pianist. Though I have no recordings of her piano playing, there are a few tunes that never fail to elicit sweet memories of hers. One is a hymn by Harry Ironside, the great twentieth-century preacher, author, and Bible teacher. The first four lines of that hymn's chorus express the blessing of being covered by the Almighty's tent:

> I'm overshadowed by His mighty love
> Love eternal, changeless pure.

Overshadowed by His mighty love
Rest is mine, serene, secure.

And the final verse of the hymn portrays the Christ-follower's stance amid the evil of this world:

Now judgment fears no more alarm,
I dread no death, nor Satan's power;
The world for me has lost its charm,
God's grace sustains me every hour.[118]

You Are Christ's Lamb

There is one last fact about you I would like to share from that passage in Revelation 7. The unidentified elder who talks with John about the great multitude in white robes tells him, "The Lamb at the center of the throne will be their shepherd; he will lead them to springs of living water."[119] What a clever turn of phrase. The Lamb is your shepherd. He is the Lamb; you are his lamb.

Phillip Keller, who applied his experience as a sheep farmer to the twenty-third Psalm in his book *A Shepherd Looks at Psalm 23*, writes:

In memory I can still see one of the sheep ranches in our district which was operated by a tenant sheep-man. He ought never to have been allowed to keep sheep. His stock were always thin, weak and riddled with disease or parasites. Again and again they would come and stand at the fence staring blankly through the woven wire at the green lush pastures which my flock enjoyed. Had they been able to speak I am sure they would have said, "Oh, to be set free from this awful owner!"

This is a picture which has never left my memory. It is a picture of pathetic people the world over who have not known what it is to belong to the Good Shepherd . . . who suffer instead under sin and Satan.[120]

You, of course, are not among those sheep that stand at the fence staring blankly through the wire at greener pastures. You are among the multitude in white robes. You are a lamb of the Lamb. The evil of this world swirls and surrounds you, but it should not confuse or confound you, for your shepherd is the Lamb of God, who takes away your sin and leads you to lush pastures and springs of living water.

Imagine how blessed you will be as you hear this message and take it to heart, like the woman Eugene Peterson writes about in his book *Reversed Thunder*:

> I was teaching this passage to a small group of people a number of years ago, and one of the members of the group, suddenly realizing its relevance, asked if she could tell her story. Years previously, she told us, she had had a nervous breakdown. Her whole life was in chaos. Nothing fit together. She could see no meaning in anything. She felt overwhelmed by evil, and guilt, and sheer bad luck. She went to a counselor and was guided by him to take a good look at each detail that she had lumped into a large pile and called "evil." Item by item the feelings and events and actions were examined. Not one of them, she said, became any less horrible or less palatable as she did that. But something else happened while she was doing it. She began to discover other items in her life that had been obscured by the great lump of piled-up wrongs: relationships that were delightful, songs that were ravishing, sights that were heart-stopping. She began to experience the wonder of her own body and how much of it was working well. She began to trust the integrity of her own feelings and

how valuable they were. She began to realize the preciousness of other lives and ways she could appreciate them. Later she came to know God, and the entire world that she now recognized in Revelation 7, came into focus for her. None of the evil was abolished, but it was all in a defined perspective. The nameless evils had names. The numberless wrongs were numbered. She was hardly aware of the point at which the proportions shifted, but now it was the good that seemed endless, and the glories that were beyond counting. Nothing in her life had changed; everything in her life was changed.[121]

May it be so for you.

Prayer

Lamb of God, who takes away the sin of the world, have mercy on me. Lord, you know the evil that surrounds me. You know how disheartening it is. You know my own struggle against evil. You know the heaviness of my heart in the face of tyranny, war, famine, death, oppression, and disaster. You know how dark and depressing this world can be. Help me, by your grace, not to be confounded by evil. Help me to focus on the realities that, according to your word, overshadow the evil of this world: I am sealed. I am connected to the vast, innumerable multitude of Revelation 7. I am pure in your sight, robed in white. I am victorious, unbowed, more than conqueror. I am your servant. I am sheltered by your tent. I am a lamb whose shepherd is the Lamb of God, who takes away my sin and leads me to lush pastures and springs of living water. Teach me to live in these realities as I await your blessed appearing. Amen.

6

Shake the Earth

Now from the altar of my heart
Let incense flames arise
                    —John Mason

Do you ever wonder if your prayers make a difference? Have you ever prayed and prayed and prayed . . . and ended up with nothing to show for it?

Have you ever used the common phrase "All we can do now is pray" and felt like that was pretty much the same as saying, "All hope is gone?"

If so, you are not alone.

In fact, I can almost guarantee you that your brothers and sisters, the Christ-followers of the first century, often felt very much the same. Because we are not the first Christians ever to feel at times like our prayers don't matter, don't amount to much, don't get answered, don't even have any apparent effect. The people to whom this book, The Revelation, was first given—those who first read it and first heard it—were suffering through a period of terror and persecution that makes our world of economic distress, environmental disaster, political chicanery, and cultural meltdown seem like *a day at the beach.* Many of these folks had managed to survive the nightmarish reign of the Emperor Nero, who brutally tortured and executed Christians. They had seen the reigns of the emperors Vespasian and his son Titus, who had killed many Jews and Christians in the Great Jewish Revolt some thirty years earlier. And the emperor Titus had been succeeded by his brother Domitian, who forced Christians to participate in the worship of the emperor or be expelled, banished, tortured, and even executed.

And so, in that context, to his people who had neither weapons nor votes, neither money nor influence against the massive engines of persecution and scorn that aligned against them, people who surely wondered if their frequent and fervent prayers had any effect, the Lord Jesus Christ gave John the apostle, who himself had been targeted by the government and banished to the island of Patmos, a vision of the prayers of the saints and their effect on the world.

When Heaven Falls Silent

The first seven chapters of The Revelation may safely be called cacophonous.

There is a loud voice like a trumpet, a voice like the roar of a waterfall. We hear praise, correction, and promises being dictated to seven churches. Thunder rumbles and peals. Four heavenly creatures cry repeatedly, "Holy, holy, holy." Twenty-four elders sing a hymn of praise to God. A mighty angel shouts, "Who is worthy to break the seals and open the scroll?" Thousands and thousands of angels sing fortissimo praises to the Lamb, until they are joined by the voice of every creature in heaven and earth. More thunderous voices. Rampaging horses. Strident martyrs' cries. Earthquake. Avalanches. Screams. An innumerable multitude of the redeemed, worshiping and singing in full voice.

After seven chapters of such rumbles and roars, John writes,

> When he opened the seventh seal, there was silence in heaven for about half an hour.[122]

Silence.

Say what?

One seal after another has been opened, with momentous effect, spilling unearthly disasters and otherworldly spectacles. And then the last seal is opened and . . . silence.

A countless multitude of white-robed, palm-waving saints: silent.

Many thousands of mighty angels: silent.

Four winged beings covered with eyes: silent.

Twenty-four elders on thrones: silent.

The sevenfold Spirit of God: silent.

The Lamb: silent.

The Enthroned One: silent.

What is that about?

I believe it has everything to do with what is about to happen. It is a silence of anticipation. A silence of expectancy. A silence of eagerness. Because what happens next is prayer. The prayers of the saints.

Why Heaven Fell Silent

John says nothing more about the silence. He doesn't interpret it. He observes it and reports it. But the reason for the silence soon seems clear from what follows.

> And I saw the seven angels who stand before God, and to them were given seven trumpets.[123]

John sees seven angels dispatched from God's throne, and each of the seven is given a "trumpet." But these are not silver or brass trumpets such as we see in orchestras or marching bands. They are shofroth, instruments made from ram's horns, like the "trumpets" that were used by Joshua and Israel at Jericho. Like those used by the priests to announce the time of the daily sacrifice at the temple and of course at the Feast of Trumpets, the annual Rosh Hashanah festival.

But, apparently, before the seven angels do anything with their shofars, another angel takes center stage:

> Another angel, who had a golden censer, came and stood at the altar. He was given much incense to offer, with the prayers of all the saints, on the golden altar before the throne. The smoke of the incense, together with the prayers of the saints, went up before God from the angel's hand.[124]

This was why heaven fell silent. This is how heaven views prayer. It is how heaven receives prayer.

Notice that the angel had a *golden* censer. It is a detail, but biblical details—and especially details in The Revelation—tend to be significant. And this is no exception. The censer is golden because of the value of its task. There was nothing more valuable to the first-century mind than gold, and there is nothing more valuable in the economy of God's kingdom than prayer.

Notice also that the angel was given "much incense" to offer along with the prayers, purifying them and ensuring their acceptability before the throne of God. The incense that was used in the tabernacle and Temple throughout Israel's history was expensive stuff. It was compounded from a detailed commandment issued by God himself.[125] Some of the ingredients had to be imported, from Arabia, for example. So the picture of "much" *heavenly* incense—as opposed to the earthly kind—indicates an impressive investment.

There could be another reason the angel was given "much incense" to offer. The incense was intended to mingle with "the prayers of *all* the saints"—eloquent and upright prayers, as well as imperfect prayers, prayers offered in weakness, and prayers that are incomplete or misguided. My prayers (which must require mounds of incense). Your prayers. They are offered with all the rest and purified with "much" heavenly incense.

Note, finally, that the comingled incense and prayers "went up before God from the angel's hand." The image strikes me. We routinely think in terms of God *hearing* our prayers (and sometimes imagine that he *hasn't* heard). But the picture of Revelation 8:4 involves more than hearing. The smoke and smell of incense mingled with the prayers, so that God saw them, smelled them, heard them, inhaled them. All of them. Perhaps in a more comprehensive way than we have ever been bold enough to imagine.

What Follows the Silence

What happens next, however, is not what we might expect. Once our prayers ascend to God's throne, we may well imagine the next scene to be pleasant, and the outcome to be positive. But that's not what happens. Not at all.

> Then the angel took the censer, filled it with fire from the altar, and hurled it on the earth; and there came peals of thunder, rumblings, flashes of lightning and an earthquake.
>
> Then the seven angels who had the seven trumpets prepared to sound them.
>
> The first angel sounded his trumpet, and there came hail and fire mixed with blood, and it was hurled down upon the earth. A third of the earth was burned up, a third of the trees were burned up, and all the green grass was burned up.
>
> The second angel sounded his trumpet, and something like a huge mountain, all ablaze, was thrown into the sea. A third of the sea turned into blood, a third of the living creatures in the sea died, and a third of the ships were destroyed.
>
> The third angel sounded his trumpet, and a great star, blazing like a torch, fell from the sky on a third of the rivers and on the springs of water—the name of the star is Wormwood. A third of the waters turned bitter, and many people died from the waters that had become bitter.
>
> The fourth angel sounded his trumpet, and a third of the sun was struck, a third of the moon, and a third of the stars, so that a third of them turned dark. A third of the day was without light, and also a third of the night.

As I watched, I heard an eagle that was flying in midair call out in a loud voice: "Woe! Woe! Woe to the inhabitants of the earth, because of the trumpet blasts about to be sounded by the other three angels!"

The fifth angel sounded his trumpet, and I saw a star that had fallen from the sky to the earth. The star was given the key to the shaft of the Abyss. When he opened the Abyss, smoke rose from it like the smoke from a gigantic furnace. The sun and sky were darkened by the smoke from the Abyss. And out of the smoke locusts came down upon the earth and were given power like that of scorpions of the earth. They were told not to harm the grass of the earth or any plant or tree, but only those people who did not have the seal of God on their foreheads. They were not given power to kill them, but only to torture them for five months. And the agony they suffered was like that of the sting of a scorpion when it strikes a man. During those days men will seek death, but will not find it; they will long to die, but death will elude them.

The locusts looked like horses prepared for battle. On their heads they wore something like crowns of gold, and their faces resembled human faces. Their hair was like women's hair, and their teeth were like lions' teeth. They had breastplates like breastplates of iron, and the sound of their wings was like the thundering of many horses and chariots rushing into battle. They had tails and stings like scorpions, and in their tails they had power to torment people for five months. They had as king over them the angel of the Abyss, whose name in Hebrew is Abaddon, and in Greek, Apollyon.

The first woe is past; two other woes are yet to come.

The sixth angel sounded his trumpet, and I heard a

voice coming from the horns of the golden altar that is before God. It said to the sixth angel who had the trumpet, "Release the four angels who are bound at the great river Euphrates." And the four angels who had been kept ready for this very hour and day and month and year were released to kill a third of mankind. The number of the mounted troops was two hundred million. I heard their number.

The horses and riders I saw in my vision looked like this: Their breastplates were fiery red, dark blue, and yellow as sulfur. The heads of the horses resembled the heads of lions, and out of their mouths came fire, smoke and sulfur. A third of mankind was killed by the three plagues of fire, smoke and sulfur that came out of their mouths. The power of the horses was in their mouths and in their tails; for their tails were like snakes, having heads with which they inflict injury.

The rest of mankind that were not killed by these plagues still did not repent of the work of their hands; they did not stop worshiping demons, and idols of gold, silver, bronze, stone and wood—idols that cannot see or hear or walk. Nor did they repent of their murders, their magic arts, their sexual immorality or their thefts.[126]

That's some freaky stuff, you must admit.
Seven blasts from seven shofars,
thunder, lightning, earthquake,
hail and fire and blood,
meteors falling from the sky,
stars and planets going dark,
deadly animals arising from the pit of Hell,
and a vicious army of two hundred million being unleashed on the earth.

The passage even mentioned Wormwood. Do you know how the word "Wormwood" is translated in many Slavic languages? *Chernobyl.* Oddly prophetic from whoever named the Ukrainian site where in 1986 a nuclear disaster rained radioactive poison throughout a vast region—much of which even today remains a no man's land of devastation. Not exactly a message of hope. Or is it?

When Prayer Re-enters History

More than any of the previous things John has seen in this revelation, chapters 8 and 9 seem to place in doubt the promise of Jesus that this is all supposed to *bless* those who read it, hear it, and take it to heart. But it is still the case, because this passage reveals to us that prayer is crucial and influential and necessary, and will become *even more so* the closer we get to the end of the world.

"*Really?*" you may ask.

"Really," I answer.

Remember, when the seventh seal was opened, there was silence in heaven for a half hour. And then the next five verses describe our prayers—*your* prayers, *my* prayers—being hand-delivered by a mighty angel of God, along with incense, to purify and beautify them. And then the vision shows the angel filling the censer with fire from the heavenly altar, and hurling it to earth, after which—with thunder, rumblings, lightning and earthquake—come seven angels with seven shofars, unleashing unspeakable horrors.

The image is meant to shock us.

In the words of Eugene Peterson,

> Prayer reenters history with incalculable effects. Our earth is shaken daily by it.[127]

Prayer shakes the earth. *Your* prayers, *my* prayers, shake the earth.

They are reverently conveyed to the throne of God by angels. They are purified with the smoke of heavenly incense. They are powered by the fire of the Holy Spirit, and *they shake the earth.*

They dispatch angels.

They resound like thunder.

They strike like lightning.

They shake the earth day after day after day!

That is the picture Jesus reveals to us in this eighth chapter of The Revelation.

Your prayers are potent. You may not feel it, you may not always see it, but The Revelation of Jesus Christ to his church through his servant John shows what happens with your prayers in heaven and what they achieve on earth.

What the Seven Shofars Mean

The vision of the angel and the golden censer is followed by the depiction of seven shofars, which— much like the seals—unleash apocalyptic destruction on the earth.

As I studied this passage several years ago with a friend, he and I wrestled with the relationship of those first five verses in Revelation 8 to the rest of chapters 8 and 9. It was a tough study. Many scholars and commentators delve into what the seven trumpets say about the horrors that will come along in the last days and precede the end of the world. But we discovered that we were pretty much on our own when it came to trying to figure out what relation this vision of the golden censer has to do with the seven shofars that follow. In other words, why did Jesus show John the angel with the golden censer right before showing him the seven angels and the seven shofars? I mean, he reveals this awesome vision of prayer and how our prayers are handled in heaven, a vision that is surely designed to motivate us and inspire us to pray . . . and then, the very

next thing, he shows seven angels with seven shofars and all kinds
of bad and freaky things happen.

Why? How are those two parts of this vision connected? Why
does one follow the other as it does? I don't know. For sure, at
least.

But I'm pretty sure it's one—and maybe all—of three possible
answers, three potential perspectives our Lord wants us to have that
will bless us if we take them to heart and that will also help us survive
the end of the world, whether it's today or ten years from now.

Pray OR . . .

It may be that Jesus shows this vision of the golden censer and the vision of seven trumpets one right after the other in order to say, "Your
prayers are beautiful and powerful . . . and so you must pray, pray,
pray, or disaster and destruction will surely come."

My wife and I love to travel in the Holy Land. One of the harder
things for us to learn was the appropriate way to make a purchase
in Israel. We had to adjust to the realization that the price marked
on a piece of merchandise was the merchant's opening bid. We were
expected to counter the offer and then to counter the seller's next offer. And so on. Not to do so, we were told, is a breach of etiquette in
that area, a disappointment and something of an embarrassment to
the seller. A shopkeeper or salesperson was not insulted by our efforts
to negotiate a better deal. Quite the contrary. They felt proud when
they made a deal that required tough negotiating. That is helpful
context for a conversation that once took place between God and
Abraham. It is related in Genesis, the first book of the Bible.

The Lord had revealed to Abraham his intention to destroy the
cities of Sodom and Gomorrah because they had become so utterly
and thoroughly wicked. So Abraham said, "What if there are fifty
righteous people living there? Will you destroy them along with the

wicked?" And God said no, he would spare the city for the sake of fifty righteous people.

So Abraham pressed the matter. He said, "What about forty-five?" God said if forty-five righteous people could be found in the city, he would spare it.

Abraham continued to haggle. What about forty? God answered the same way.

And so it went. Thirty? Twenty? As few as *ten*? And God said he'd spare the city for the sake of just ten righteous people. As it turned out, however, there weren't even *that* many. Those cities were apparently a lot like Washington, D.C.

Maybe Jesus revealed this heavenly vision of prayer before the sounding of the seven shofars to encourage us to intercede like Abraham. Perhaps part of the ministry of these chapters to us is to get us praying, or else things like this are sure to come. It could be that the message of these chapters is that your prayers may prolong the day of grace.

But there is a second possibility.

Pray THAT . . .

It may be that Jesus shows this vision of the golden censer and the vision of seven trumpets one right after the other in order to say, "Your prayers are beautiful and powerful . . . so you must pray *in order to bring about these things.*"

It seems like a really harsh message, but it does seem like the prayers of the saints and the fire from the altar, when they are hurled to the earth by the angel, actually *activate* the things that follow.

You know, for thousands of years, the righteous have cried out to God,

> How long will the enemy mock you, O God?
> Will the foe revile your name forever?[128]

And just two chapters earlier in this revelation, when the fifth seal was opened, we heard the souls of Christian martyrs crying out,

> "How long, Sovereign Lord, holy and true, until you judge the inhabitants of the earth . . . ?"[129]

So it may be that the message Jesus wants us to hear is, "Pray . . . *so that* God's justice will come."

That may be hard for us to believe . . . maybe because we live in relative comfort. We have food, shelter, air-conditioning, Krispy Kreme donuts. Our lives, even on our worst days, are fairly enjoyable compared to our brothers and sisters who lived during the reign of Domitian—or who today live in the Sudan or Saudi Arabia or North Korea.

Youcef Nadarkhani is an Iranian man who became a Christian at an early age. He subsequently became a pastor leading a network of house churches in the Islamic Republic of Iran. In December 2006, he was arrested on charges of apostasy, because government officials claimed that he had converted from Islam to Christianity (Nadarkhani, who was born to Muslim parents, says he never practiced Islam). The court also charged him with the crime of evangelizing Muslims. He was released two weeks later.

In October 2009, he learned that the Iranian government would require the school his two young sons attended to teach Islam. Pastor Nadarkhani protested to the school, citing the Iranian constitution, which allows freedom of religion. Shortly thereafter, Nadarkhani was arrested and charged with protesting (the charges were later changed to apostasy and evangelizing Muslims). He has been imprisoned since then.

Pastor Nadarkhani was tried in September 2010, found guilty, and given a death sentence.[130] He was transferred to a prison for political prisoners and denied all access to his family. He has faced repeated efforts to persuade or coerce him into renounce Christianity and convert to Islam (his wife was also arrested and imprisoned for four months, an apparent effort to pressure Nadarkhani).

In February 2012, news outlets around the world reported that Iranian authorities had issued an order to execute Pastor Nadarkhani. An international outcry ensued, and Iranian officials later denied the reports.[131] As of this writing, Nadarkhani continues to be imprisoned but (despite reportedly poor health) has remained steadfast.

Many followers of Jesus live in similar circumstances. For those enduring oppression and persecution and extreme hardship, the message to "pray . . . *so that* God's justice will come" would be a powerful and encouraging message to hear. In other words, the message of Revelation 8 and 9 may be that your prayers may usher in the day of justice.

But there is one more possibility.

Pray BECAUSE . . .

It may be that Jesus shows this vision of the golden censer and the vision of seven trumpets one after the other to say, "Your prayers are beautiful and powerful . . . so you must pray *because* these things are coming."

Whether it happens tonight or tomorrow or ten years or a hundred years from now, God's Word warns us that cataclysm and catastrophe are coming. Such things are in our future. Such things are in this world's future.

So whatever else we may do, why would we *not* do what is beautiful and powerful in God's sight? Why would we not dispatch angels with our prayers? Why would we not roar like thunder and flash like lightning? Why would we not shake the earth with the power of our prayers?

Whatever else Jesus is saying to us today, we can be utterly confident that he is saying: *pray.*

Pray because your prayers are beautiful and powerful.

Pray because these things are coming.

Pray because your prayers will align you with God's will for you and for your world.

If the world should end tonight, I can think of nothing better I should be doing than praying.

If the world doesn't end until next week, I can think of nothing better I should be doing between now and then than praying.

If the coming of the Lord is still a long ways off, I can think of nothing better I should be doing in the meantime than praying.

The friend with whom I studied these chapters, John Johnson, captioned the message of Revelation 8 and 9 this way:

> Our prayers mix with the actions of God . . .
> to bring about the will of God.

So pray . . . because there is nothing better you can do to survive the end of the world. There is nothing better you can do for this life today, for whatever awaits you tomorrow, for whatever this cruel world may throw at you in the future . . . than to pray. I hope that message is real to you. I hope it inspires you to pray. Because whatever else Jesus is saying to us through Revelation 8 and 9, I believe he is saying: pray.

Prayer

Oh, my Lord, whether my prayers will prolong the day of grace or usher in the day of justice, I know they will align me with your will for me and my world. I know they will bless you and bless me. I know there is nothing better I can do for this life today, for whatever awaits me tomorrow, for whatever this world may throw at me in the future than to pray. So I pray, Lord.

I pray for those who don't yet know "the boundless riches of Christ."[32]

I pray for those who even now are facing persecution—even martyrdom—for the sake of the Gospel.

I pray for those who cry to heaven for deliverance.

I pray for those who will be afflicted by the evils that are soon to come upon this earth.

Lord, hear my prayer. Let this prayer shake the earth, dispatch angels, roll like thunder, and strike like lightning. And make me faithful beyond this moment, beyond this day, to shake the earth with my prayers of faith, in Jesus' name, amen.

7

Salt of the Earth

He comes, he comes,
Judge so severe;
Seven trumpets speak,
Oh, they speak him near
        —American Gospel Song

My wife is a professional counselor. She loves her job and is extremely good at it. She works with children and adults, families and the aged. She possesses a seemingly bottomless well of compassion and patience for people who are hurting. She is unfazed by people with the most severe dysfunctions (which explains how she agreed to marry me). She accepts the ups and downs of people with addictions with a calm dignity. She is unruffled by wild mood swings and angry threats. On one occasion, a new client told her not to make any sudden moves or she would risk being punched; that person soon became one of my wife's most appreciative clients.

But there is one aspect of her job she doesn't enjoy. In fact, it's worse than that. She dreads it. Because she works with children and families, many of whom are facing difficult situations, she is often required to testify in court. Though she is articulate in speech and impressive in appearance, she worries about every court appearance. She knows it is an honor to give her professional opinion to the court, but she fears she might say the wrong thing or give the wrong impression. And, since her testimony is often influential in families staying together or children being removed from abusive situations, she knows a lot is riding on it.

Her situation is not unlike yours. Or mine.

Last-Minute Reminders

As strange and mysterious as it is, The Revelation Jesus gave to the church through his beloved disciple John touches on themes that are important—or should be—to every follower of Christ. The voice of Jesus. Truth and error. Love and faithfulness. Worship. Prayer. The fear and frustration that comes from being surrounded—and even oppressed—by evil.

The reader or listener who can step back and take a broad, thoughtful view of these unveilings (the literal meaning of the book's title in Greek), without getting bogged down in the frequently overwhelming symbols and allusions, may see a chronology of events, as bestselling authors Tim Lahaye and Jerry Jenkins do, with great drama and detail, in their Left Behind series of novels. But it's possible to see something else, something more like a wise parent's admonishment than a historian's timeline.

From the time my children started attending school and on through their teenage years, my wife would see them off to school with a short prayer and a few words of advice. In their earliest years, the advice might have been "Keep your lunch money in this pocket until lunchtime" or "Give this note to your teacher." Later, in their teens when they went on dates or outings with friends, the advice became something of a mantra, which our children can repeat to this day (though they are now parents themselves). It went something like this: "No smoking, drinking, drugs, or sex, and remember who you belong to" (meaning, of course, God). Eventually, I added, "And don't drive faster than thirty-five miles per hour" to the formula—only half-joking. And, though it became an inside joke in our family, it never lost its original meaning. Those words as the kids went out the door were last-minute reminders of important things we wanted them to remember.

I truly believe it is possible to read The Revelation as something like that. Last-minute reminders of the truly important things, especially in light of the approaching End of All Things.

Grasp the Importance of Giving a Wise Witness

In that light, chapters 10 and 11 of The Revelation emphasize the importance of Gospel proclamation and Christian witness in the End Times. Chapter 10 opens with yet another "mighty angel" appearing to the Apostle John (not one of the angels with the shofars referred to throughout chapters 8 and 9, but another like the "mighty angel" who earlier proclaimed in a loud voice, "Who is worthy to break the seals and open the scroll?"[133]):

> Then I saw another mighty angel coming down from heaven. He was robed in a cloud, with a rainbow above his head; his face was like the sun, and his legs were like fiery pillars. He was holding a little scroll, which lay open in his hand. He planted his right foot on the sea and his left foot on the land, and he gave a loud shout like the roar of a lion. When he shouted, the voices of the seven thunders spoke. And when the seven thunders spoke, I was about to write; but I heard a voice from heaven say, "Seal up what the seven thunders have said and do not write it down."[134]

The appearance of this angel forms another interlude between the blowing of the sixth and seventh shofars, like the vision of the great multitude that preceded the opening of the seventh seal. Unlike that part of the vision, however, John is no longer an observer. He will soon become a participant.

The "seven thunders" that are prompted by the angel's shout may be a reference to Psalm 29, often called "The Psalm of the Seven Thunders," in which David describes the voice of the Lord in terms like that of a violent thunderstorm. The angel, however, tells the Apostle John not to write what the thunders speak. But the angel doesn't say why.

It could be that the time was not right. Maybe the world was not ready for that part of the vision. Perhaps it was for John's ears only. We don't know. We won't know, presumably, until the end of all things, when "we will see everything with perfect clarity."[135]

In any case, Eugene Peterson helps us to apply the angel's words to John:

Witness, apparently, does not mean telling everything we see and hear, breathlessly and indiscriminately. Reticence is as much a part of witness as expression. Jesus, descending from the Mount of Transfiguration with the three disciples, instructed them "tell no one the vision" (Matt. 17:9), not because it must never be known, for it came to be known, but because that was not the right time. There are numerous instances in Jesus' life when he forbade those who were healed to tell about it. This was not because they had been initiated into a secret society, but because they were being trained in the exacting and difficult Christian skill of witness, in which there is "a time to keep silence and a time to speak" (Eccl. 3:7).[136]

This is a crucial message for those of us living in the twenty-first century. Your witness is critical, just as John's was. The contrast between the "mighty angel" and the aged John could not have been greater. The angel wore a cloud for a robe and a rainbow for a crown. He straddled land and sea. His shout was like the roar of a lion. Yet John—like you—was God's chosen messenger. He would write (or not write) the vision, as he was commanded. And though we may not know all the reasons or all the details, we are likewise entrusted with the message of God and the angels. No follower of Jesus is so small or insignificant that his or her witness can be neglected—especially in the last days.

But it cannot be an indiscriminate witness. We must be wise. We are "like sheep among wolves,"[137] and so we must be shrewd. Our words must be "always full of grace, seasoned with salt,"[138] "making the most of every opportunity, because the days are evil."[139]

Grasp the Privilege and Pain of Your Witness

After telling John to refrain from recording the message of the seven thunders, the angel next swears an oath and makes an ominous announcement:

Then the angel I had seen standing on the sea and on the land raised his right hand to heaven. And he swore by him who lives for ever and ever, who created the heavens and all that is in them, the earth and all that is in it, and the sea and all that is in it, and said, "There will be no more delay! But in the days when the seventh angel is about to sound his trumpet, the mystery of God will be accomplished, just as he announced to his servants the prophets."

Then the voice that I had heard from heaven spoke to me once more: "Go, take the scroll that lies open in the hand of the angel who is standing on the sea and on the land."

So I went to the angel and asked him to give me the little scroll. He said to me, "Take it and eat it. It will turn your stomach sour, but in your mouth it will be as sweet as honey."' I took the little scroll from the angel's hand and ate it. It tasted as sweet as honey in my mouth, but when I had eaten it, my stomach turned sour. Then I was told, "You must prophesy again about many peoples, nations, languages and kings."[140]

When John is told to take the scroll, he approaches the mighty angel and asks to be given it. But the angel repeats the command: "Take it." John is no longer permitted to be a passive observer of the events that are taking place in heaven and on earth; he is called to participation. So he takes the scroll and eats it, as the angel commanded. And just as the angel said, the scroll tastes sweet in his mouth but turns bitter in his stomach.

It is a striking image, which John's first readers would have recognized as echoing words written centuries earlier by the prophet Ezekiel:

He told me, "Son of man, eat what you see. Eat this book. Then go and speak to the family of Israel." As I opened my mouth, he gave me the scroll to eat, saying, "Son of man, eat this book that I am giving you. Make a full meal of it!" So I ate it. It tasted so good—just like honey.

Then he told me, "Son of man, go to the family of Israel and speak my Message. . . . But . . . they won't listen to you because they won't listen to me. They are, as I said, a hard case, hardened in their sin. But I'll make you as hard in your way as they are in theirs. I'll make your face as hard as rock, harder than granite. Don't let them intimidate you. Don't be afraid of them, even though they're a bunch of rebels."

Then he said, "Son of man, get all these words that I'm giving you inside you. Listen to them obediently. Make them your own. And now go. Go to the exiles, your people, and speak. Tell them, 'This is the Message of God, the Master.' Speak your piece, whether they listen or not."

Then the Spirit . . . lifted me and took me away. I went bitterly and angrily.[141]

So it is. Although my wife is honored as a counselor to speak on behalf of children and families in difficult situations, it is often an onerous task she must undertake when she is called upon. Every follower of Jesus is called to "eat this book," as the Spirit said to Ezekiel, and the angel to John. It is a privilege and a joy, sweet like honey. But with the privilege comes also a responsibility, and that is often laced with bitterness.

There are some, of course, who find it easy to witness to the hope that is in them. And some, because of their impressive gifts or long practice, experience great success as they testify to the things God has done in and for them. But easy or not, sweet or bitter, every Christ-follower is Ezekiel, so to speak. Every one of us is John. Each of us is called and commanded to "eat this book" and "get all these words inside you" and then to go and speak, "whether they listen or not."

It is a joy. And it is a burden. Sweet and sour. But no true follower of Jesus is denied the privilege and pain of witnessing to the grace of our Lord Jesus Christ—especially in light of the approaching End of All Things.

Grasp How Dangerous Your Witness Is

It would be one thing if witnessing to the life-changing power of God in Christ were only occasionally inconvenient to us or sometimes annoying to others. But it is more than that. It is quite another thing, as the eleventh chapter of The Revelation makes clear. John reports further:

> I was given a reed like a measuring rod and was told, "Go and measure the temple of God and the altar, with its worshipers. But exclude the outer court; do not measure it, because it has been given to the Gentiles. They will trample on the holy city for 42 months. And I will appoint my two witnesses, and they will prophesy for 1,260 days, clothed in sackcloth." They are "the two olive trees" and the two lampstands, and "they stand before the Lord of the earth." If anyone tries to harm them, fire comes from their mouths and devours their enemies. This is how anyone who wants to harm them must die. They have power to shut up the heavens so that it will not rain during the time they are prophesying; and they have power to turn the waters into blood and to strike the earth with every kind of plague as often as they want.
>
> Now when they have finished their testimony, the beast that comes up from the Abyss will attack them, and over-

power and kill them. Their bodies will lie in the public square of the great city—which is figuratively called Sodom and Egypt—where also their Lord was crucified. For three and a half days some from every people, tribe, language and nation will gaze on their bodies and refuse them burial. The inhabitants of the earth will gloat over them and will celebrate by sending each other gifts, because these two prophets had tormented those who live on the earth.[142]

Revelation 11 is considered by some scholars and students of the Bible to be the most difficult and important chapter in the entire book. It is central to the book, and some interpreters see in its nineteen verses a summary or outline of all that follows.

It starts with John being told to measure the temple. Since The Revelation was received and written decades after the temple in Jerusalem had been demolished by Roman armies, it is clear that the temple is a symbol, as well as an echo of Ezekiel's and Zechariah's prophecies. In John's vision, the temple represents the church, the people of God, who, though subject to persecution in the last days, are represented also by two witnesses.

Many interpreters of The Revelation take the reference to "two witnesses" literally. And they may be right. As the end approaches, there may be two messengers from God who preach in sackcloth and work wonders for three and a half years before being killed. Or the two witnesses may be more symbolic than that, representing the end-times witness of all true followers of Jesus.

In any case, it seems crystal clear that being a true witness to the existence of God, the truth of the Gospel, and the power of God for salvation is and will be an increasingly dangerous proposition in the days that precede the end of the world as we know it.

In recent years, atheism has become a more aggressive—and antagonistic—ideology. Militant opposition to Christianity regularly makes widows, orphans, slaves, and martyrs of Christians. Even democratic nations are sometimes overt in their efforts to suppress Christian witness and discriminate against Christians. Some employers, municipalities, and organizations intentionally make it difficult to be a professing and practicing Christian. Christians in academia sometimes face discrimination. Today's world can be a dangerous place for the witnessing Christian.

But your witness is not only dangerous to you. It is dangerous to others as well. That is, perhaps, why the Gospel can elicit such opposition from others. The Revelation says of the two prophets depicted in chapter 11 that they "had tormented those who live on the earth."[143] Your witness can be a torment—a threat—to those who are far from God. That reality doesn't excuse you from your responsibility to be wise and discerning and full of grace in your living and speaking, but it should remind you not to be surprised or discouraged when people "insult you, persecute you and falsely say all kinds of evil against you" because of your witness, "for in the same way they persecuted the prophets who were before you."[144]

Grasp How Unconquerable Your Witness Is

Significantly, the story of the two witnesses does not end with their death. Like Lazarus, whom Jesus called out of an earthly tomb, they return to life—not on the third day, like Jesus, but on the fourth day:

> But after the three and a half days the breath of life from God entered them, and they stood on their feet, and terror struck those who saw them. Then they heard a loud voice from heaven saying to them, "Come up here." And they went up to heaven in a cloud, while their enemies looked on.
>
> At that very hour there was a severe earthquake and a tenth of the city collapsed. Seven thousand people were killed in the earthquake, and the survivors were terrified and gave glory to the God of heaven.
>
> The second woe has passed; the third woe is coming soon.[145]

Whether you agree with those who think the two witnesses are actual individuals to appear in the last days or with those who see them as symbolic of the witnessing church—or something else—this much is clear and worthy of emphasis: what the destruction of the seals and trumpets failed to accomplish, the martyrdom and vindication of God's faithful witnesses did. "The survivors were terrified and gave glory to the God of heaven."[146]

Those words should stun us. Particularly after the cataclysmic events described in the chapters leading up to them: Tyranny and war. Famine and disease. Oppression and disaster. Earthquake, hail, wildfire, volcanic eruptions, falling meteors, global warfare. And to what effect?

> The rest of mankind who were not killed by these plagues still did not repent of the work of their hands; they did not stop worshiping demons, and idols of gold, silver, bronze, stone and wood—idols that cannot see or hear or walk. Nor did they repent of their murders, their magic arts, their sexual immorality or their thefts.[147]

But two witnesses clothed in sackcloth (symbolizing repentance) and filled with the Spirit of God (indicated by the reference to them as "the two olive trees and the two lampstands"), who end up being murdered and humiliated, prompt those around them to give glory to the God of heaven.

Just so. No matter how ill-equipped you are, no matter how ineffectual you may feel, your witness is unconquerable. Like the two witnesses described in Revelation 11, the Lord will keep your lamp burning; with his help, you can have a greater impact than that of earthquakes and armies.[148]

I believe it is significant that that message to you and to me precedes the seventh trumpet, or shofar, in the Revelation of Jesus Christ to his servant John. Because that vision of the importance, privilege, pain, danger, and invincibility of our witness ought to prompt us to join in the praise and worship that concludes Revelation 11:

The seventh angel sounded his trumpet, and there were loud voices in heaven, which said:

"The kingdom of the world has become
the kingdom of our Lord and of his Messiah,
and he will reign for ever and ever."

And the twenty-four elders, who were seated on their thrones before God, fell on their faces and worshiped God, saying:
"We give thanks to you, Lord God Almighty,
the One who is and who was,
because you have taken your great power
and have begun to reign.
The nations were angry,
and your wrath has come.
The time has come for judging the dead,
and for rewarding your servants the prophets
and your people who revere your name,
both great and small—
and for destroying those who destroy the earth."

Then God's temple in heaven was opened, and within his temple was seen the ark of his covenant. And there came flashes of lightning, rumblings, peals of thunder, an earthquake and a severe hailstorm.[149]

Like the angels in heaven, we ought to give praise and thanks to God for the sweet privilege that is ours to witness—and, if he decides, to suffer—for him. Though it may be costly, it is an honor and a blessing.

Prayer

I give thanks to you, Lord God Almighty, the One who is and who was, because you have taken your great power and have begun to reign. I give praise and thanks to you for the privilege that is mine to witness to your kindness, to your beauty, to your great salvation. I confess that it is both privilege and pain to me—sweet and bitter. I ask you, please, to make me faithful to speak at your urging and to refrain at your prompting. Light my lamp, and keep it burning. Make my witness bold and unconquerable, reminding me that by your grace and in your strength I can have a greater impact than that of earthquakes and armies. Amen.

8

All the King's Horses

Though the ancient dragon rage,
And call forth all his host to war,
Though earth's self-righteous sons engage
Them and their god alike I dare;
Jesus, the sinner's friend, proclaim;
Jesus, to sinners still the same
— Charles Wesley

My first attempt to drive in Europe went well. Probably because I was following someone from Frankfurt to Herborn, Germany. Subsequent trips, however, didn't go as well. It had to do with the signs.

Accustomed as I am to driving in the United States, my internal navigation system relies a lot on a sense of whether my destination is north, south, east, or west from my current location. Happily, in North America, highway signs typically indicate not only the next large city in a particular direction, but they actually identify the general compass point: I-75 North, for example, will get you from London (Kentucky) to Lima (Ohio), and I-94 West will get you from Paw Paw to Paw Paw Lake in Michigan.

But I discovered that's not how it works in southwest Germany and northeast France. There, you pretty much have to know which direction Karlsruhe or Colmar is before you make a turn. If your intended destination isn't listed on the highway sign at an interchange, you may end up in Gruppenbadenfriederbergen instead of Lorsquevous Avez Voulu-aller. And you don't want that. Trust me.

Signs are important. They can let you down. They can lead you on. And sometimes, they can get you where you want to go.

That is true, of course, of signs of the end times. Jesus said there would be signs—in the sun, moon, and stars, among the nations and in the sky.[150] He told his followers to be alert for those signs.[151] The signs are there, in the Bible. All we have to do is look.

Still, some of us can't help but struggle with the length, breadth, and depth of The Revelation and, rather than being prompted to spend more time reading our Bibles, we just want someone to boil it down for us into bite-sized chunks, the way the network newscasts and *USA Today* often do it. With that in mind, this is as good a time as any to present my take on . . .

The Top Ten Signs the Apocalypse Is Near

10. Snooki (of *Jersey Shore* fame) published a book. With real words in it.
9. The Centers for Disease Control published a paper on how to prepare for a Zombie Apocalypse. No, seriously, they did.
8. Bigfoot has his own reality TV show.
7. The latest cosmetic surgery fad: the "vampire facelift."
6. Hollywood actually made a good movie last year.
5. Barney the dinosaur now wears a hooded black cape and carries a big ol' scythe.
4. Cockroaches are building little tiny bleachers all over the place to watch the end when it comes.
3. Your GPS announces "Right turn. Now approaching . . . Apocalypse."
2. Uncle Harvey's trick knee is acting up something awful.

And the number one sign of the approaching apocalypse:

1. McDonald's sign reads "Over 666 billion sold."

Okay, so I may have made up the last five or six of those. But some of them are true, although they probably aren't really signs of the apocalypse. Still, the signs *do* seem to be all around us. It does seem like the whole world is going to pot—acts of terrorism, collapsing banks, bankrupt nations, freakish weather, environmental disasters, and on and on. It can seriously leave the people of God wondering, "What's going on?" and "What does it mean?" and "How am I supposed to respond?"

And if we look to the twenty-two chapters of The Revelation

for answers to those questions, we might come away feeling more confused than before. There are so many possible interpretations of the mysterious symbols and events in the Apostle John's record of the visions he received as an exile on the island of Patmos. But I truly believe it is not necessary to try to understand or explain every detail and make it all fit together in a way that makes sense to us. I think it is far more important to focus on the reason the Bible says this revelation was given to us—to *bless* us and to prepare us for whatever the world and the devil may throw at us, now or in the future.

A Holy End-Times Perspective

I hope you have been blessed and prepared already by what The Revelation says about you, your relationship to Jesus, your worship, your posture towards evil, your call to prayer, and your witness. It is important that all those things come before the portion of Scripture we will explore in this chapter, because we desperately need to hear from God about those things before we can possibly arrive at a holy end-times perspective on such things as politics, world history, and religion—which is what chapters 12, 13, and 14 of The Revelation cover.

As we do so, it is also important to remember that the people who were the first to receive, hear, and read this book, The Revelation, were suffering through a period of terror and persecution that makes the confusing and disturbing politics, culture, and religion of our day seem mild by comparison. And so our Lord—through John—responded to those severe times by showing his first-century followers—and now, through his recorded Word, us—three revealing perspectives to adopt (in chapters 12 and 13) and by giving them and us (in chapter 14) a new vision of three redeeming practices to apply.

Adopt Three Revealing Perspectives

Chapter 12 through chapter 14 of The Revelation, the last book in the Bible, is one of the most intriguing passages in all of Scripture. It features images and characters that would challenge the ability of any science fiction writer or special effects designer: a woman clothed with the sun, a dragon with seven heads, Michael the archangel and his armies, a beast emerging from the sea, a second beast arising from the earth, and more. This cycle of visions follows the seven seals and seven trumpets, precedes the seven bowls, and provides us . . .

A Cosmic Perspective of History

Most people think we have two separate nativity accounts in Scripture: Matthew's account, which includes the story of the Magi, and Luke's report, which features the shepherds. But we actually have three. Revelation 12 is the cosmic perspective not only of the birth of Jesus but of the focal point of human history. It says,

> A great and wondrous sign appeared in heaven: a woman clothed with the sun, with the moon under her feet and a crown of twelve stars on her head. She was pregnant and cried out in pain as she was about to give birth.[152]

Now, this is metaphor. This is symbolism. The woman is the people of God. Israel. The children of Abraham, the nation that gave birth to the Messiah.

> Then another sign appeared in heaven: an enormous red dragon with seven heads and ten horns and seven crowns on his heads. His tail swept a third of the stars out of the sky and flung them to the earth.[153]

The dragon is Satan, and the heads and horns and crowns signify power. The reference to him sweeping a third of the stars out of the sky is a depiction of the day long ago when the mighty Archangel Lucifer led many of his fellow angels in a heavenly rebellion against God and thus became God's adversary (the meaning of the word "Satan") and ours. It is not prophecy but history. It refers not to the future but to the past. The account continues:

> The dragon stood in front of the woman who was about to give birth, so that he might devour her child the moment it was born. She gave birth to a son, a male child, who will rule all the nations with an iron scepter. And her child was snatched up to God and to his throne. The woman fled into the desert to a place prepared for her by God, where she might be taken care of for 1,260 days.[154]

Those verses describe, in a mere eighty-one words, the birth of Jesus, the "male child," his resurrection and ascension and the subsequent dispersion, or *diaspora*, of the Jews, who from AD 70 until 1948 were expelled and exiled from their promised land but never forgotten by God, who amazingly preserved them as a people and restored them as a nation. Then, verse 7 continues,

> And there was war in heaven. Michael and his angels fought against the dragon, and the dragon and his angels fought back. But he was not strong enough, and they lost their place in heaven. The great dragon was hurled down—that ancient serpent called the devil, or Satan, who leads the whole world astray. He was hurled to the earth, and his angels with him.
>
> Then I heard a loud voice in heaven say:
>
> "Now have come the salvation and the power

and the kingdom of our God,
and the authority of his Christ.
For the accuser of our brothers,
who accuses them before our God day and night,
has been hurled down.
They overcame him
by the blood of the Lamb
and by the word of their testimony;
they did not love their lives so much
as to shrink from death.
Therefore rejoice, you heavens
and you who dwell in them!
But woe to the earth and the sea,
because the devil has gone down to you!
He is filled with fury,
because he knows that his time is short."[155]

Then, in the final verses of chapter 12, this dragon who tried to destroy the child turns again to pursue the woman, and not only her
but "the rest of her offspring"—that is, you and me, "those who hold
to the testimony of Jesus."

That is the perspective of history we must have. It is God's perspective. Everything in history relates, in one way or another, to the
grand drama of the dragon and the "male child" and the people of
God.

That is what matters. *That* is the focal point of history, and
the final scene of that great drama is where all subsequent history points. It is a perspective we need in order to survive these
apocalyptic times in which we live. It is a perspective that will
align us with God's view of history and arm us against panic, fear,
compromise, and surrender.

But it's not the only perspective we need.

A Chilling Perspective of Politics

You have enemies. Many enemies. Revelation 12 introduced the dragon, a powerful and sinister enemy. Chapter 13 begins,

> And the dragon stood on the shore of the sea.
> And I saw a beast coming out of the sea. He had ten horns and seven heads, with ten crowns on his horns, and on each head a blasphemous name. The beast I saw resembled a leopard, but had feet like those of a bear and a mouth like that of a lion. The dragon gave the beast his power and his throne and great authority.[156]

John sees in his vision a great sea monster, like the Leviathan described in the book of Job, rising from the sea with heads and horns and crowns just like his master, the dragon. And the subsequent verses describe this beast's maneuverings in the world, his power and authority over every tribe, people, language, and nation.

This is a revealing perspective of politics. Some Bible students think this "beast" is a man, the Antichrist, Satan's right-hand man in the Last Days. And maybe it is. But it is also a chilling perspective for Christ-followers of any age, as it shows the wickedness and ugliness that accompanies the politics of this world.

The politics of this world require the exercise of power, even brutality, and it is a temptation of the church to use the world's weapons to accomplish heaven's goals. John's vision of the sea beast ought to show us how futile that idea is. As Paul writes to the Corinthians, we do not live by the standards of this world:

> For though we live in the world, we do not wage war as the world does. The weapons we fight with are not the weapons of the world. On the contrary, they have divine power to demolish strongholds. We demolish arguments and every pretension that sets itself up against the knowl-

edge of God, and we take captive every thought to make it obedient to Christ.[157]

Our weapons are powerful and numerous. Such as faith, which can move mountains.[158] And prayer, a weapon which, when it is wielded by a righteous man or woman, "availeth much."[159] And kindness, which triumphs over judgment.[160] And, of course, love, which is the greatest of Christian virtues,[161] and the mightiest weapon of all. These are the weapons that demolish strongholds and defeat arguments. Not the weapons of the world. Not contention. Not deceit. Not ridicule, slander, or threats.

Followers of Jesus still—and always—face the temptation (as Jesus himself did in the wilderness[162]) to wage heaven's war with earthly weapons. But it cannot be done. It will only end up hurting us and our cause. That doesn't mean it will be easy. The world's weapons are deadly, no doubt about it. And they will be aimed at you.

But don't be fooled. Don't be naïve. Don't be surprised when the powers of this world chew you up and spit you out. That is why John's vision of political power is called a "beast." That is why verse 10 tells us,

> This calls for patient endurance and faithfulness on the part of the saints.[163]

Our enemy, the dragon of chapter 12, will use the politics of this world—the politics of your nation, your state, your community, and your workplace, to imprison and destroy, to bring about captivity and conflict, and to lead you and me astray—because, remember, it's the woman of chapter 12 and her "other offspring" he wants to destroy, and that includes you and me. So we need that perspective of the way this world operates.

But we need more than that.

A Critical Perspective of Religion

A second beast follows hard on the heels of the first in John's vision. This land beast is similar to the sea beast, but it bears its own distinguishing marks:

> Then I saw another beast, coming out of the earth. He had two horns like a lamb, but he spoke like a dragon.[164]

This land-beast is like the Behemoth described in the book of Job, but with an important and striking difference: it has two horns like a lamb. Notice, *like* a lamb.

In other words, it is a counterfeit. It is a fake. An imposter.

It has two horns *like* a lamb, but it speaks like its master, the dragon. And the following verses in chapter 13 show a revealing perspective of this world's religion:

> It exercised all the authority of the first beast on its behalf, and made the earth and its inhabitants worship the first beast, whose fatal wound had been healed. And it performed great signs, even causing fire to come down from heaven to the earth in full view of the people. Because of the signs it was given power to perform on behalf of the first beast, it deceived the inhabitants of the earth. It ordered them to set up an image in honor of the beast who was wounded by the sword and yet lived. The second beast was given power to give breath to the image of the first beast, so that the image could speak and cause all who refused to worship the image to be killed. It also forced all people, great and small, rich and poor, free and slave, to receive a mark on their right hands or on their foreheads, so that they could not buy or sell unless they had the mark, which is the name of the beast or the number of its name.[165]

Many interpreters think this "beast" is also a man, "the false prophet," a kind of evil high priest in the Last Days. And that may well be so.

But it is also a critical perspective for Christ-followers of any age, as it paints a hideous picture of the religion of this world. Its object is to get us to worship, but *not* to worship the Lamb—*any*thing but the Lamb. But it is all deception.

Notice how the religion of this world is fueled by money, getting people to buy and sell at its bidding. This is scary, because the picture painted in Revelation 13 is of a commercialized, market-driven, prosperity-seeking religion that is all too common in our day and in our country . . . and, God save us, in the church.

So don't be misled. Don't be deceived by the religion of this world. Don't chase the commercial cult of the second beast.

That is why verse 18 tells us,

> This calls for wisdom. If anyone has insight, let him cal-
> culate the number of the beast, for it is man's number.
> His number is 666.[166]

"It is man's number." 666 is the number of a *human*. The religion of this world will *imitate* the divine, but it is 666, a triple failure to be 777, a number that would indicate perfection, completion, divinity.

As Eugene Peterson says,

> This religion has nothing to do with God. Get its num-
> ber: it is a *human* number. This is not divine mystery, but
> a confidence man's patter: it is religion that makes a show,
> religion that vaunts itself, religion that takes our eyes off
> of the poor and suffering and holy Christ.[167]

These are the perspectives we need in the end times. These are perspectives we need at *all* times.

I think too much end-times teaching focuses on straw men and bogeymen. Too much of it steers too close to superstition and sensationalism. But what if we understand the spirit of Antichrist not solely as a "Doctor Evil" character but as the way we do politics, the way we treat people, the way we attain power and exercise power?

And what if the second beast is the godless, powerless religion that so many tune into, that so many settle for—religion that makes a show, religion that vaunts itself, religion that takes our eyes off of the poor and suffering and holy Christ?

This calls for patient endurance and faithfulness. This calls for wisdom. This calls for qualities that are sorely lacking in much of the church, in many of us, in me. Which is why I not only need to adopt these three revealing perspectives, I also need to . . .

Apply Three Redeeming Practices

The transition from chapters 12 and 13 to chapter 14 could not present a more jarring contrast if the soundtrack were to suddenly change from death metal music to the soaring strains of Handel's *Messiah* . . . which it kind of does:

> Then I looked, and there before me was the Lamb, standing on Mount Zion, and with him 144,000 who had his name and his Father's name written on their foreheads. And I heard a sound from heaven like the roar of rushing waters and like a loud peal of thunder. The sound I heard was like that of harpists playing their harps. And they sang a new song before the throne and before the four living creatures and the elders. No one could learn the song except the 144,000 who had been redeemed from the earth. These are those who did not defile themselves with women, for they kept themselves pure. They follow the Lamb wherever he goes. They were purchased from among men and offered as firstfruits to God and

the Lamb. No lie was found in their mouths; they are blameless.[168]

What a striking departure. After the vision of the dragon, the sea beast and the land beast, suddenly John sees the Lamb and a multitude of the redeemed worshiping him.

This is what I need to do. This needs to be *my* practice. And yours.

While the dragon is pursuing, while the sea beast is oppressing, while the land beast is deceiving, I need to be worshiping. That's how to survive the end of the world. That is the first of three redeeming practices God's Word shows me:

Worship, for Redemption Has Come!

Notice the contrast in the opening verses of Revelation 14 with the "mark of the beast" mentioned earlier. Those worshiping the Lamb have his name and God's name written on their foreheads. I believe that's the people of God. That's you and me.

We have his name written on us.

We sing a new song.

We follow the Lamb wherever he goes.

We have been purchased, redeemed.

We are blameless in God's eyes.

Why wouldn't we worship? That's a redeeming practice we need to apply to ourselves and carry out in our lives. And so is what John sees next:

> Then I saw another angel flying in midair, and he had the eternal gospel to proclaim to those who live on the earth— to every nation, tribe, language and people. He said in a loud voice, "Fear God and give him glory, because the hour of his judgment has come. Worship him who made the heavens, the earth, the sea and the springs of water."
>
> A second angel followed and said, "Fallen! Fallen is Bab-

ylon the Great, which made all the nations drink the mad-
dening wine of her adulteries."

A third angel followed them and said in a loud voice:
"If anyone worships the beast and his image and receives
his mark on the forehead or on the hand, he, too, will
drink of the wine of God's fury, which has been poured
full strength into the cup of his wrath."[169]

This, too, is how to survive the end of the world, the second of three
redeeming practices God's Word shows me through John's vision:

Spread the Gospel, For Judgment Is Coming!

The first angel, or messenger, has the eternal gospel, the Gospel we
are called and commissioned to proclaim. The other angels pro-
nounce judgment.

It is so easy in this crazy, runaway world to get wrapped up in history as it's being made, in politics and all the worry and fear it causes,
in today's commercialized, market-driven, prosperity-seeking religion.
But John's vision points us to what is truly urgent and important. It
reminds us to spread the Gospel, because judgment is coming.

Our neighbors and friends and families are all being victimized
by the dragon and the beasts of politics and religion. They are ex-
posed to judgment, and we're sitting on our cans.

This calls for patient endurance on the part of the saints who
obey God's commandments and remain faithful to Jesus.[170]

Absolutely it does! Judgment is coming, whether Jesus comes tomorrow or not, and I want my friends and loved ones to escape condem-
nation and wrath just as I have. I want them to survive the end of the
world, just as I will.

So let's spread the word. Let's share the joy. Let's proclaim the day
of salvation to everyone we can.

Which leads to the last of three redeeming practices God's Word shows me.

Hurry, For the Harvest Is Near!

Imagine the elderly John, who was born and raised in Galilee, who had watched Jesus die in Jerusalem, who was a leader of the church as it soon after became a movement of thousands, who lived and wrote and preached in Ephesus, who mentored Polycarp (who later became bishop of Smyrna) and then was exiled to the island of Patmos. Imagine the hundreds—maybe thousands—of people he knew and loved in Galilee, Jerusalem, Ephesus, and Asia Minor. Imagine all that, and then read what John saw next, and recorded in Revelation 14:

> I looked, and there before me was a white cloud, and seated on the cloud was one "like a son of man" with a crown of gold on his head and a sharp sickle in his hand. Then another angel came out of the temple and called in a loud voice to him who was sitting on the cloud, "Take your sickle and reap, because the time to reap has come, for the harvest of the earth is ripe." So he who was seated on the cloud swung his sickle over the earth, and the earth was harvested.
>
> Another angel came out of the temple in heaven, and he too had a sharp sickle. Still another angel, who had charge of the fire, came from the altar and called in a loud voice to him who had the sharp sickle, "Take your sharp sickle and gather the clusters of grapes from the earth's vine, because its grapes are ripe." The angel swung his sickle on the earth, gathered its grapes and threw them into the great winepress of God's wrath. They were trampled in the winepress outside the city, and blood flowed out of the press, rising as high as the horses' bridles for a distance of 1,600 stadia.[171]

That's a sobering end to a dizzying passage of this Revelation. It must certainly have given John pause. And it should do the same for us.

Five or so years ago, I got a call at about 2:30 a.m. from the woman who is now my daughter-in-law, Nina. She told me my son Aaron, on his way home from her house, had been in an accident and that I should come.

I jumped in the car, of course, and raced up Route 177. I saw the police on the scene, and the car he had been driving smashed into a tree by the side of the road. I parked my car in a driveway. As I approached the scene, I was looking, looking, looking through the darkness sliced by the pulsing lights of the police cruiser for my son. I finally saw him lying flat on the ground. A cloth of some kind covered him.

There are no words to describe what I felt right then.

I ran to him and knelt next to him on the pavement. My heart must have started again when I saw that he was alive, and conscious. And, while he was in shock, he had only broken a wrist and banged himself up pretty good.

I soon learned that he had swerved to avoid a deer in the road and had still been going quite fast when he hit the tree head-on. But I'll never forget the sight of his form on the pavement.

I was so afraid time had run out. So afraid I'd spoken my last words to him without knowing it. So afraid.

I don't want time to run out for anyone I know. I don't want it to run out for you or for anyone you love and care about.

John's vision ought to place everyone you know under that blanket on that pavement, in your mind's eye. It ought to remind you that the harvest is near. Time is short. It will soon run out.

Whatever else The Revelation says, it says that. And whatever else we might take to heart from it, we must be sure that our sins are forgiven and the Lamb of God is alive in our hearts. And then we must make sure that we do all we can to help those around us do likewise, for the harvest is near.

Prayer

Amen, Lord. I worship you, for redemption has come to my little soul. I will spread the Gospel, with your help, for I know that judgment is coming. And I will waste no more time, for I know the harvest is near, and I want everyone around me to experience forgiveness, regeneration by the Holy Spirit, and life everlasting, in Jesus' name, amen.

9

Here Comes the Judge

Who shall not fear Thee, Lord,
And magnify Thy Name?
Thy judgments, sent abroad,
Thy holiness proclaim
                    —Henry Ware, Jr.

R.E.M. is an American rock band formed in 1980 when Michael Stipe and Peter Buck met in a record store. They had their first mainstream hit in 1987, the same year the song "It's the End of the World as We Know It" appeared on their album *Document*.

The song begins, "That's great, it starts with an earthquake," and the rest of the words fly by fast and furiously, mentioning birds and snakes, hurricane, fire, book burning, and . . . cheesecake. Like I said, the words fly by pretty fast. But you didn't really think we would make it through a book entitled *How to Survive the End of the World* without mentioning R.E.M.'s song, did you?

But there's a reason for mentioning it. That song, whether you love it or hate it, crystallizes many people's impressions about the end of the world: it's going to be a time of chaos, most people think. Bedlam. Pandemonium. The worldwide equivalent of a bench-emptying hockey brawl. But it ain't necessarily so.

God Is Not Sleeping

It is really easy in our day to look around and see so much that is wrong with our world . . . no less than our brothers and sisters of the first century, when John's vision was written down and circulated among the churches he knew and loved. We see wars and oppression, disease and starvation, filth and pollution, economic exploitation, you name it.

And at times it seems, even to the most faith-filled among us, that God is asleep at the switch, as our world careens toward destruction. But the testimony of the Bible—and the message of The Revelation—is that God is *not* sleeping. It says,

God isn't late with his promise as some measure lateness. He is restraining himself on account of you, holding back the End because he doesn't want anyone lost. He's giving everyone space and time to change.[172]

But the Bible is also clear that there *will* come a day when the space and time to change will come to an end . . . and no one knows exactly when. The Bible says it will come as a "thief in the night."[173] But, in the meantime, The Revelation of Jesus Christ given to us through his servant John has a message intended to bless us as we read it and take it to heart. And for all of us who have grieved over humanity's ugliness and this world's harshness, Revelation 15–18 has three urgent and important messages.

Don't Be Distracted from Worship

Time after time, in this revelation, Jesus shows John a vision of heavenly worship.

Time after time, Jesus turns John's attention to the worship of saints and angels and the twenty-four elders and heavenly beings.

Before the Lamb opens the first of the seven seals, he shows John a throne in heaven and angels and living creatures worshiping around the throne.

Before he sends forth the angels with the seven trumpets, he shows John a great multitude in white robes, worshiping before the throne.

Before an angel with a sickle is sent out to harvest the souls of men, Jesus shows the 144,000 again and the four living creatures and the twenty-four elders singing their worship to the Lamb.

And then, just before seven bowls of God's wrath pour out seven plagues of judgment on the earth (in Revelation 16), John is shown this:

> I saw in heaven another great and marvelous sign: seven angels with the seven last plagues—last, because with

them God's wrath is completed. And I saw what looked like a sea of glass mixed with fire and, standing beside the sea, those who had been victorious over the beast and his image and over the number of his name. They held harps given them by God and sang the song of Moses the servant of God and the song of the Lamb:

"Great and marvelous are your deeds,
Lord God Almighty.
Just and true are your ways,
King of the ages.
Who will not fear you, O Lord,
and bring glory to your name?
For you alone are holy.
All nations will come
and worship before you,
for your righteous acts have been revealed."

After this I looked and in heaven the temple, that is, the tabernacle of the Testimony, was opened. Out of the temple came the seven angels with the seven plagues. They were dressed in clean, shining linen and wore golden sashes around their chests. Then one of the four living creatures gave to the seven angels seven golden bowls filled with the wrath of God, who lives for ever and ever. And the temple was filled with smoke from the glory of God and from his power, and no one could enter the temple until the seven plagues of the seven angels were completed.[174]

Time after time, Jesus reveals the interconnectedness of worship with events on earth and the unfolding of the End Times. I believe it is for a purpose. I believe part of the message of The Revelation is: Don't be distracted from worship.

With everything going on in this unique book of the Bible—thunders and lightnings, earthquakes and meteors, men and nature and angels all going at each other—heaven's worship goes on, un-abated, uninterrupted, unimpeded.

And so should ours. So should yours. So should mine.

Sure, it's easy to be distracted. The news comes on first thing in the morning with reports of bombs going off and hurricanes approaching and people dying, and the radio waves are filled with talking heads arguing back and forth, and you just have to shake your head at the latest gossip at the water cooler or in the halls of academia. It's unbelievable sometimes. Unfathomable. Unsettling.

But the message of The Revelation is this: don't let any of that distract you from what really matters. And the worship of God, the focus of *your* heart and will and mind and voice on the being and action of the one true God, is what really matters.

So, yes, the world is going to pot. Yes, our culture is corrupt. Yes, things may be getting worse in many ways, but that is *all the more reason* to sing and pray and listen to God in worship. I believe that's what Revelation 15 says to us. Whatever else it might say, it says that.

Don't let the tragedies of the past or the threats of the present impede your worship of him who is, who was, and who is to come. Whatever is wrong with the world, don't be distracted from worshiping all that is right in him . . . with all that is in you.

Don't Be Discouraged by Injustice

I can't imagine that anyone who becomes familiar with the Bible can fail to see the amazing attention to theme and detail that characterizes it. These chapters of The Revelation are no exception. Chapter 15 depicted a victorious heavenly choir singing the Song of Moses and of the Lamb, praising the Lord God Almighty for his holy ways and righteous acts. Then chapter 16 begins,

> Then I heard a loud voice from the temple saying to the seven angels, "Go, pour out the seven bowls of God's wrath on the earth."[175]

Then follows a series of judgments on the people of the earth,
  from painful sores
  to the sea and rivers and springs turning to blood,
  to intense, burning heat from the sun,
  and then darkness,
  and then the River Euphrates drying up,
  and finally a cataclysmic earthquake accompanied by hail.
There is a clear correspondence between these plagues and the plagues visited on Egypt.

You see, when Moses first went to Pharoah to ask him to "let my people go,"[176] the purpose was for them to hold a festival in the wilderness. Moses' appeal was for Pharoah to set them free . . . to worship.

But, of course, Pharoah responded negatively. He challenged God's authority and said, "Nothin' doin'"—or the Egyptian equivalent thereof—and so God sent plagues on the Egyptians until the Hebrews were not only set free to worship in the wilderness but to become a nation of their own.

Yet here, in a similar—not identical, but similar—scenario, a series of plagues are poured out. And, while the angels and saints respond by praising God's justice, the people of the earth—like Pharoah—"cursed the name of God, who had control over these plagues, [and] . . . refused to repent and glorify him."[177]

And as it was with Pharoah, so it is with the people in John's vision; the worse things get, the more they curse God and refuse to repent, as Revelation 16:11 and 16:21 emphasize:

> People gnawed their tongues in agony and cursed the God of heaven because of their pains and their sores, but they refused to repent of what they had done.[178]
>
> And they cursed God on account of the plague of hail, because the plague was so terrible.[179]

We see those things today.

I mean, come on, can so-called reality TV get any more depraved? Can the "angry atheists" become any more unhinged? Who doesn't feel like common sense and common decency are nowhere to be found in the halls of government, the houses of entertainment, or the havens of academia?

I know God never promised his people a rose garden, but doesn't it seem to you that some of the best people lose their jobs, the wrong people get sick, the nicest people go through the worst things? For crying out loud (literally), there are more people in slavery today than at any other time in history. Christians are being tortured and killed for their faith—and, to many, it's not even newsworthy. Children die every day from abuse, and only the most sensational such stories are even noted. And if you watch the news or read the paper—or pay even the slightest attention—it can get downright overwhelming.

But the message of God's Word for us today is this: don't get discouraged by injustice. God's wrath *will* be poured out. Justice *will* come, as Paul promised the church at Thessalonica:

> Justice is on the way. When the Master Jesus appears out of heaven in a blaze of fire with his strong angels, he'll even up the score by settling accounts with those who gave you such a bad time. His coming will be the break we've been waiting for.[180]

Justice will not be denied. It is sure. And when it comes, the angels will say,

> You are just in these judgments,
>> you who are and who were, the Holy One,
>> because you have so judged;
> for they have shed the blood of your saints and prophets,

and you have given them blood to drink as they deserve."[181]

And the very altar of heaven will respond,
"Yes, Lord God Almighty,
true and just are your judgments."[182]

Every soul who has been hurt will be healed. All crime, abuse, all hatred and perversion and ugliness will be punished in the bowls of God's wrath.

So don't be discouraged by injustice. It will be put right. God's wrath will be poured out, and his justice will be served on all the earth—in such a way as to make angels sing.

Don't Be Deceived by Excess

I hope you realize that the Bible is not a bunch of feel-good platitudes and fairy tales. If you haven't before this moment, I hope you will discover that fact—and never forget it—as you look at Revelation 17 and 18.

Our God is not afraid to tell it like it is, and those two chapters show John—and us—a disturbing vision of excess and cruelty, in the depiction of a woman riding a beast in the first verses of Revelation 17. The beast is the land beast we met in chapter 13, which corresponds to religion and religious deception. But the woman is making her first appearance.

> Then the angel carried me away in the Spirit into a desert. There I saw a woman sitting on a scarlet beast that was covered with blasphemous names and had seven heads and ten horns. The woman was dressed in purple and scarlet, and was glittering with gold, precious stones and pearls. She held a golden cup in her hand, filled with abominable things and the filth of her adulteries. This title was written on her forehead:

MYSTERY
BABYLON THE GREAT
THE MOTHER OF PROSTITUTES
AND OF THE ABOMINATIONS OF THE EARTH.

I saw that the woman was drunk with the blood of the
saints, the blood of those who bore testimony to Jesus.[183]

To John's first audience—the followers of Jesus in Ephesus, Smyrna, Pergamum, and other places, perhaps, throughout the Roman Empire—the identity of the woman was probably crystal clear. She is Rome. The name, "Babylon the Great," equates that ancient city's evil with the contemporary wickedness of Rome—luxurious, lustful, corrupt, violent, imperial Rome. John's first readers certainly would have seen Rome in these verses and, in the verses to follow, veiled references to Roman emperors (including the current one) and more emperors who were to come.

Some contemporary readers and scholars (called *preterists*) hold the opinion that the first-century understanding was and is correct; in other words, they see the events of chapters 17 and 18 being fulfilled in the years immediately following the reign of Domitian, leading up to the Fall of Rome in 476. Others have seen in the woman and the beast a depiction of the last days in terms that mirror Babylon and Rome. Many Protestant interpreters have identified the woman as the Roman Catholic Church—which, of course, is headquartered in Rome. Others see in the woman on the beast an unholy alliance of world government and world religion that will gain ascendance in the Last Days.

If you find all the possible interpretations to be too confusing, don't worry. You don't have to be a Bible scholar or an expert on eschatology (the study of the End Times) to be blessed by and take heart from Revelation 17–18. Because whatever historical or prophetic meaning the woman and the beast have (or don't have), it is quite certain that these chapters depict this world's idolatry and corrupt value system in alliance with each other. And, whether we're talking about the late first century or the early twenty-first century (or a time yet to come), such idolatry and excess infect the whole world, as verse 15 explains:

> Then the angel said to me, "The waters you saw, where the prostitute sits, are peoples, multitudes, nations and languages."[184]

The idolatry and excess of this world will always make war with the true church, the universal, worldwide company of those who follow Jesus, just as ancient Babylon imprisoned the ancient Jews and ancient Rome persecuted the first Christians (which may be why this woman is equated symbolically with both Rome and Babylon).

But it will not always be so. Revelation 18 promises that. It describes the fall of Babylon the Great—announced by angels, sung by a voice from heaven, and mourned by the inhabitants of the earth—until the chapter closes:

> Then a mighty angel picked up a boulder the size of a large millstone and threw it into the sea, and said:
>
> "With such violence
>> the great city of Babylon will be thrown down,
>> never to be found again.
> The music of harpists and musicians, flute players and trumpeters,
>> will never be heard in you again.
> No workman of any trade
>> will ever be found in you again.
> The sound of a millstone
>> will never be heard in you again.
> The light of a lamp

> will never shine in you again.
> The voice of bridegroom and bride
>   will never be heard in you again.
> Your merchants were the world›s great men.
>   By your magic spell all the nations were led
> astray.
>   In her was found the blood of prophets and of the
> saints,
>   and of all who have been killed on the
> earth."[185]

The message of those verses, perhaps among many other meanings and themes, is that all the pomp and circumstance, all the prideful positioning and extravagant luxury of this world's excess. . . .

All the twisted, crazy, backward things we see day after day, where hungry children pull decaying food out of a trash heap while just miles away a government "servant" eats a $500 spoonful of caviar. . . .

The upside-down value system where we measure a man by what he makes, where people become celebrities by sleeping with someone, where we make a girl feel fat if she's not emaciated like the pictures in magazines, where we turn the faith that was once-for-all delivered to the saints, for which martyrs have died, into a Fortune 500 company that sells Jesus t-shirts and trinkets. . . .

Someday all that will be brought down by God. Someday he will restore godly values and righteous standards once more on this earth.

Don't be deceived by such excess. We are too often, too easily, and too willingly deceived by the same things this world is deceived by.

Don't be.

Revelation 17 and 18 assure us that this world's idolatry and corrupt value system will be judged by God.

You will not then, nor do you now, need Abercrombie and Fitch to tell you what looks good.

You will not then, nor do you now, need a diamond to feel loved (or to make your wife feel loved).

You will not then, nor do you now, need anything but God's saving grace to make you acceptable in his sight.

So don't be distracted from worship; it's too important.

Don't be discouraged by injustice; God's justice is coming.

And don't be deceived by excess; unless it's an excess of passion and devotion and commitment to God.

Prayer

Almighty God, I praise you that you will soon cast down all the injustice and excess that surrounds me and mine. Thank you for the promise of deliverance from these pervasive evils.

In the meantime, help me not to be fooled. Help me not to be discouraged by injustice or deceived by excess. But, most of all, help me not to be distracted from worship, for you alone are worthy, holy, and triumphant. Great and mighty are your deeds. Just and true are your ways. I bow before you in body, mind, and spirit. I worship you, holy and just God, in Jesus' name, amen.

10

The Wedding and the War

Bride of Christ, whose glorious warfare
Here on earth hath never rest;
Lift thy voice, and tell the triumphs
Of the holy and the blest
    —Jean B. de Contes; trans. John Ellerton

Mac Sledge is a washed up, alcoholic country music star who, after meeting Rosa Lee, a soldier's widow trying to raise her son by herself, resolves to quit drinking and try to start over. Under the influence of Rosa Lee's kindness and faith instead of alcohol, Mac is baptized along with her son, Sonny. Afterward, when Sonny asks Mac if he feels any different, he answers, "Not yet." But he is changing. He marries Rosa Lee. He begins attending church. And, when a fan of his music asks him, "Were you really Mac Sledge?" he responds, "Yes, ma'am, I guess I was."

Delmar is an escaped convict traveling with his fellow escapees Pete and Everett when they encounter a procession of singing, white-robed souls gathering at the river for a baptism. Pete and Everett watch in amazement as Delmar bolts into the river and splashes to the head of the procession, where the preacher speaks a few words and then baptizes him.

"Well that's it, boys. I've been redeemed. The preacher's done warshed away all my sins and transgressions. It's the straight and nar-row from here on out, and heaven everlasting's my reward."

Everett protests. "Delmar, what are you talking about? We've got bigger fish to fry."

"The preacher says all my sins is warshed away, including that Piggly Wiggly I knocked over in Yazoo."

"I thought you said you was innocent of those charges," Everett counters.

"Well I was lyin'. And the preacher said that that sin's been warshed away too. Neither God nor man's got nothin' on me now. C'mon in, boys. The water is fine."

Debrah's drug addiction has destroyed her marriage and alienated her from her family and from the church where she once sang in the choir. From all appearances, her addiction will soon claim her life. But, one Sunday, as her daughter sings her first solo with the church choir, Debrah enters the packed church from the back and launches into a heartfelt plea of her own, singing, "Just as I am, I'm in need of the blood of the Lamb, oh, my soul says, 'yes!'" Her husband greets her. Her daughter goes to her. And she is wrapped in their arms as if they are the arms of her Savior.

Perhaps you've recognized the movies in which those three scenes appear: 1983's *Tender Mercies*, the 2000 comedy, *O Brother, Where Are Thou?*, and Tyler Perry's 2005 movie, *Diary of a Mad Black Woman*. Each of these movies depicts salvation a little differently, and yet in my short lifetime I've seen salvation come to a human soul in much the same way as these Hollywood depictions. Maybe you have, too.

As interesting and moving as those screen depictions of salvation may be, the book of Revelation in the Bible contains a portrayal of salvation unlike any of those—and probably unlike any depiction of salvation you've ever seen.

A Four-Hallelujah Chorus

Revelation 19 and 20 provide us with a heavenly view of salvation, one that is simultaneously inspiring and challenging.

Maybe you have grown up as I have, with certain images of "salvation" in your mind's eye. Chances are, they are images that resemble how you came to experience the saving grace of God in Christ. Maybe you picture a person coming forward in a church service and kneeling at an altar. Perhaps your picture involves a soul at its lowest point, finally giving in to the Spirit of God and crying out in tearful repentance. Or maybe it's a soldier in a foxhole. Or a child at her bedside. Or something else.

Whatever images in your mind's eye are associated with salvation, The Revelation probably presents a strikingly different picture—a picture, remember, that follows Revelation 15–18, in which we saw God putting a righteous end to injustice and excess in this world, as summarized in the seven bowls of God's wrath being poured out and in the decisive destruction of the woman on the beast, the one called Babylon, the "Great Whore," as the King James Version calls her.[186]

And so, as God's judgment is meted out on the world, finally, decisively, the nineteenth chapter of this Revelation begins with the words,

After this I heard what sounded like the roar of a great multitude in heaven shouting:

"Hallelujah!
Salvation and glory and power belong to our God,
      for true and just are his judgments.
He has condemned the great prostitute
      who corrupted the earth by her adulteries.
He has avenged on her the blood of his servants."

And again they shouted:

"Hallelujah!
The smoke from her goes up for ever and ever."

The twenty-four elders and the four living creatures fell down and worshiped God, who was seated on the throne. And they cried:

"Amen, Hallelujah!"

Then a voice came from the throne, saying:

"Praise our God,
>   all you his servants,
>   you who fear him,
>   both small and great!"

Then I heard what sounded like a great multitude, like
the roar of rushing waters and like loud peals of thunder,
shouting:

"Hallelujah!
>   For our Lord God Almighty reigns."[187]

You've heard of the Hallelujah Chorus, right? That refrain in Handel's
Messiah: "Hallelujah! For the Lord God omnipotent reigneth"?

This is where those words come from, except that, if you look
carefully at Revelation 19, you'll see that this is not a "Hallelujah
Chorus." It is actually a "Four-Hallelujah Chorus." Count 'em.

Verse 1: "a great multitude" shouts, "Hallelujah!"

Verse 3: "the multitude" shouts again, "Hallelujah!"

Verse 4: the twenty-four elders and four living creatures cry,
"Hallelujah!"

Verse 6: a great multitude again shouts, "Hallelujah!"

And what is it that has heaven so worked up?

Salvation.

God has destroyed sin and corruption. He has crushed injustice
and excess. He has ended the mistreatment of his people. He has put
everything right.

Right now, here and now, he is doing that person by person, soul
by soul, and it is often a subtle and a slow process. But there is coming
a time, perhaps not too far from now, when God will work salvation
globally. Decisively. Instantly. For all to see. And all the saints, all the
angels, all the powers of heaven will shout, "Hallelujah!" to see it.

Chapter 19 of The Revelation shows us two scenes that represent this great salvation, scenes that have much more to teach us than a movie—even the best movie—depictions not only of what is to come, but also of what is—or should be—now. They are two challenges, two invitations, two calls, for every one of us to hear and heed.

Come to the Wedding

After the heavenly Four-Hallelujah Chorus, the heavenly multitude continues shouting, with these words, beginning in verse 7:

> "Let us rejoice and be glad
>   and give him glory!
> For the wedding of the Lamb has come,
>   and his bride has made herself ready.
> Fine linen, bright and clean,
>   was given her to wear."
> (Fine linen stands for the righteous acts of the saints.)
>
> Then the angel said to me, "Write: 'Blessed are those who are invited to the wedding supper of the Lamb!'" And he added, "These are the true words of God."
>   At this I fell at his feet to worship him. But he said to me, "Do not do it! I am a fellow servant with you and with your brothers who hold to the testimony of Jesus. Worship God! For the testimony of Jesus is the spirit of prophecy."[188]

The picture presented here is of a wedding feast.

In John's day, as in Jesus' day, a wedding was not a ceremony and a reception of a few hours, as it is in many Western cultures today. It was a week-long affair. It could even go on longer.

On the first day of the wedding, the bride would wait, seated on an elaborate throne, for her bridegroom to come. He would come, accompanied by his father, her father, and the whole guest list, dancing and singing, and when he arrived he would come to her and place over her head a fine linen veil. Then he would lead her to the chuppah, the canopy of love, where they would exchange vows, and then, the wedding completed, the feast would begin.

And it would go on . . . and on . . . and on . . . as long as seven days or more.

That is a picture of salvation.

My salvation.

Your salvation.

Jesus Christ, the Son of God, offers to bind himself to me . . . and to you. And when we accept his proposal, he pledges his eternal, undying, unchanging love so that whoever is joined to him can escape the burden and penalty of sin and receive the free gift of eternal life.

This is why the Bible calls Jesus the bridegroom, and the church is called his bride.

John the Baptist was once asked how he felt about the fact that Jesus was gaining more popularity than John, the one who had introduced him. John said,

> I told you, 'I am not the Messiah. I am only here to prepare the way for him.' It is the bridegroom who marries the bride, and the best man is simply glad to stand with him and hear his vows. Therefore, I am filled with joy at his success.[189]

Another time, Jesus was asked why his followers did not fast, as did the Pharisees and the disciples of John. Jesus said,

> Do wedding guests mourn while celebrating with the groom? Of course not. But someday the groom will be taken away from them, and then they will fast.[190]

And Paul, the great first-century church planter, compared his ministry to the church at Corinth to that of a *shadchan*, a Jewish matchmaker:

I feel a divine jealousy for you, since I betrothed you to one husband, to present you as a pure virgin to Christ.[191]

Jesus is the bridegroom. And he calls you and me to come to the wedding; he will come to you where you are, and he will give you *his* righteousness, as a Jewish groom gives a veil of fine linen, bright and clean, to his bride to wear.

Oh, don't miss the importance of that picture. It is saturated with deep, deep meaning. It tells you that salvation comes to you not by you *deserving* something or *learning* something or *performing* something. It comes when you *accept* something.

Sometimes in my church, the receiving of communion and the giving of our tithes and offerings are scheduled as a two-part action. For example, rather than having ushers pass plates or offering bags down each row of seats, we have sometimes had large buckets or receptacles at the front of the auditorium so that as people come forward to receive communion they can also bring their offerings forward as an act of worship. However, on those occasions, I have usually instructed people to receive communion first, before giving their offering. I explain that the order is important, because the Lord's table is a preview of the wedding feast of the Lamb. Each of us receives God's grace before we have anything to give to him. Salvation must be received before our sacrifices are acceptable—not the other way around.

No matter who you are, no matter what your past, whether you were a drunken country music star, an escaped convict, a drug addict—or something else—if you have experienced the salvation of God in Christ, it was because Jesus came to you. You may have come forward in a church service, but that was after Jesus came to you. You may have knelt by your bedside, but that was after Jesus came to you.

Whether you knew it at the time or not, he came, dancing and singing. He found you, where you were. He placed over your head a fine linen veil. He led you under his canopy of love, and there he announced to one and all that you belonged to him. He pledged himself to you forever. Then, like a Jewish bridegroom crushing a glass goblet under his feet, he crushed your past and all the power of sin under his feet—and the angels cried and sang for joy.

And believe it or not, that is only the beginning. There will yet come a day when the best and most beautiful, the most joyful and extravagant wedding you've ever been to will pale—utterly pale—in comparison to your feasting and partying in God's presence, at the wedding feast of the Lamb.

But between now and then, the story goes on. The Revelation goes on, because the remainder of chapter 19 and on into chapter 20 of The Revelation shows us the second of the two challenges, two invitations, two calls, I mentioned earlier.

Go Out to War

After the beautiful vision of the wedding feast, a vision so over-whelming that John the apostle fell to his knees at the feet of the angel who's been showing him all these things, there is a startling, shocking turn in the vision, from a wedding . . . to a war.

> I saw heaven standing open and there before me was a white horse, whose rider is called Faithful and True. With justice he judges and makes war. His eyes are like blazing fire, and on his head are many crowns. He has a name written on him that no one knows but he himself. He is dressed in a robe dipped in blood, and his name is the Word of God. The armies of heaven were following him, riding on white horses and dressed in fine linen, white and clean. Out of his mouth comes a sharp sword with which to strike down the nations. "He will rule them with an iron scepter." He treads the winepress of the fury of the wrath of God Almighty. On his robe and on his thigh he has this name written:
>
> KING OF KINGS AND LORD OF LORDS.

And I saw an angel standing in the sun, who cried in a loud voice to all the birds flying in midair, "Come, gather together for the great supper of God, so that you may eat the flesh of kings, generals, and mighty men, of horses and their riders, and the flesh of all people, free and slave, small and great."

Then I saw the beast and the kings of the earth and their armies gathered together to make war against the rider on the horse and his army. But the beast was captured, and with him the false prophet who had performed the miraculous signs on his behalf. With these signs he had deluded those who had received the mark of the beast and worshiped his image. The two of them were thrown alive into the fiery lake of burning sulfur. The rest of them were killed with the sword that came out of the mouth of the rider on the horse, and all the birds gorged themselves on their flesh.[192]

Chapter 20 goes on from there. It tells you that *you will reign with Jesus* a thousand years, on this earth, like the Pevensee children in the Chronicles of Narnia. Here is how C. S. Lewis depicts it in the final chapter of *The Lion, the Witch and the Wardrobe*:

> Next day was more solemn. For then, in the Great Hall of Cair Paravel—that wonderful hall with the ivory roof and the west wall hung with peacock's feathers and the eastern door which looks towards the sea, in the presence of all their friends and to the sound of trumpets, Aslan solemnly crowned them and led them to the four thrones amid deafening shouts of, "Long Live King Peter! Long Live Queen Susan! Long Live King Edmund! Long Live Queen Lucy!"
>
> "Once a king or queen in Narnia, always a king or queen. Bear it well, Sons of Adam! Bear it well, Daughters of Eve!" said Aslan.

And through the eastern door, which was wide open, came the voices of the mermen and the mermaids swimming close to the shore and singing in honor of their new Kings and Queens.

So the children sat on their thrones and scepters were put into their hands and they gave rewards and honors to all their friends. . . . And they made good laws and kept the peace and saved good trees from being unnecessarily cut down, and liberated young dwarfs and young satyrs from being sent to school, and generally stopped busybodies and interferers and encouraged ordinary people who wanted to live and let live. . . . And they entered into friendships and alliance with countries beyond the sea and paid them visits of state and received visits of state from them.[193]

The Chronicles of Narnia is fantasy, of course. But your future reign is reality. And that future reality includes also the fact that Satan will then be bound and judged and utterly destroyed, and every wicked deed will be judged, and death and hell themselves will be destroyed.

But, until that time, you are in a battle, a real and grueling war. Eugene Peterson says, in his book *Reversed Thunder*,

> The moment we walk away from the [Lord's table], having received the life of our Lord, we walk into Armageddon, where we exercise the strength of our Lord.[194]

The two go together. The wedding and the war.

I know, I know, we want sweetness and light. We want comfort and luxury, even. We want the blessings of salvation, not the struggles of warfare. We want "Happy those who trust in Jesus, Sweet their portion is, and sure."[195] Not "Onward Christian soldiers, marching as to war."[196]

But we can't have one without the other. They are two essential pictures of salvation, two sides of the same coin, two lenses in the same pair of spectacles. That's at least part of what Revelation 19 and 20 make clear to us.

There *will* come a day, of course, when all will be put right, and sorrow and grief will cease, and struggle will end—but that day ain't yet. And here, and now, the moment we receive from our gracious and loving Lord, we walk into Armageddon, where we must learn to exercise the strength of our Lord. Peterson also points out the similarity between this vision of salvation and the night on which Jesus was betrayed; he enjoyed the feast and then left for the agony of the garden and the struggle on the cross. First the meal, then the battle.

You cannot accept salvation and avoid struggle. You cannot say "yes" to Jesus and "no" to his cause. You cannot receive eternal life and then go on vacation. You cannot follow Christ and avoid the struggle between good and evil.

If that is what you're doing, then you must rethink your picture of salvation. In fact, if that is what you're doing, be very careful about calling yourself a Christian. Because *salvation makes us warriors . . .* or we have not experienced salvation.

To quote Eugene Peterson again:

> Salvation, then, is not simply something that God does: it is something that God is doing, and not only for us but with us, enlisting us in the saving action.[197]

Front and Back

I sincerely and fervently hope that you have received the salvation of our Lord Jesus Christ, by grace through faith. If you haven't, then the fact that you're reading this means it is not too late. So, I'd like to give you something, and encourage you to accept it prayerfully and wholeheartedly:

The Royal Invitation

His Majesty, the King of the Universe, requests the honor of your presence at the Royal Wedding of the Ages (Rev. 19:7) between Yeshua Ha Mashiach (Jesus), His only begotten Son, and His Bride, the called-out ones.

You are cordially invited to partake in the Marriage Supper of the Lamb by being cleansed in His blood (Heb. 9:14), which He shed for your salvation (Heb. 2:14).

By pledging your heart (Rom. 10:9-10) to His plans and purposes for your life, He promises to lead (Rom. 8:14) and guide you in the ways of truth (John 16:13), provide for all your needs, physically and spiritually (Matt. 6:32-34), shower you with gifts (1 Cor. 12:1-10; Romans 12:6-8) by His Ruach Ha Kodesh (Holy Spirit), with whom He will fill you (Joel 2:28-29; Eph. 5:18), and wash you in the water of His Word (Eph. 5:25-26) so that you may be used (2 Tim. 3:16) to tell others about this glorious feast.

As a token of His love for you, you will be given a veil of fine linen, bright and clean, covering you with his righteousness (Rev. 19:8) as He rejoices over you, His bride (Isa. 62:5), and clothes you in the wedding garments of salvation and righteousness (Isa. 61:10).

"Who in his or her right mind would refuse an invitation like that? But it has a "flip side" to it. The other side of your invitation looks like this:"

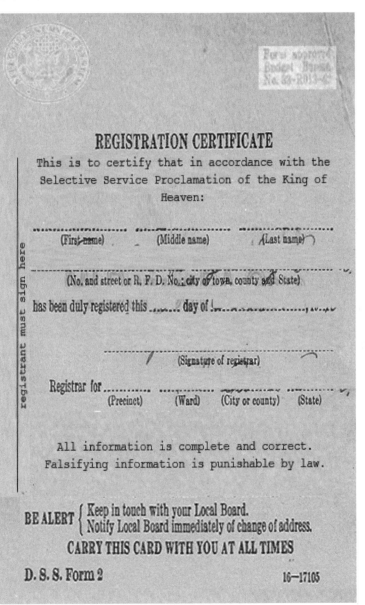

REGISTRATION CERTIFICATE

This is to certify that in accordance with the Selective Service Proclamation of the King of Heaven:

(First name)　(Middle name)　(Last name)

(No. and street or R. F. D. No.; city or town, county and State)

has been duly registered this ...... day of ....

(Signature of registrar)

Registrar for ....
(Precinct)　(Ward)　(City or county)　(State)

All information is complete and correct. Falsifying information is punishable by law.

BE ALERT { Keep in touch with your Local Board.
Notify Local Board immediately of change of address.

CARRY THIS CARD WITH YOU AT ALL TIMES

D. S. S. Form 2　　　　16—17105

Obviously, that is not an invitation. It is a draft card, much like those carried by young men of previous generations. This one is not filled out. It requires your information. It needs your signature.

If you have accepted the invitation, I encourage you to go ahead and sign the draft notice. Because it "comes with," as some would say. You are even welcome to photocopy these pages and print your wedding invitation and draft card back to back and carry it with you to remind you of the end-times reality in which you (and I) live.

No One Gets a "Plus-One"

Let me share one more thought with you.

In first-century Jewish marriage customs, the bride's family did not attend the wedding feast. That may be hard to picture, but I'm told it was the custom. The wedding feast was the joyful celebration of the groom and the groom's family at receiving the bride into their midst.

Let me say it again, because it is important. The bride's family did not attend the wedding feast.

That means, when John the Apostle saw in a vision the wedding feast of the Lamb, first-century people would have had an understanding of that event which most twenty-first-century people lack. They would have understood that the bride's family members were not participants. They were not guests. They were not invited. It just wasn't done.

In other words, we must be the bride, or we will not be there. We must be the bride.

Take just a moment to wrap your head around that truth.

We must be the bride. Not related to the bride. Not descended from the bride. Not a friend, much less a friend of the family. The bride. Only the bride herself, among all the bride's people, comes to the feast.

This is why the wedding and the war are inseparable. No one

comes to the wedding feast on the bride's coattails. No one gets a "plus one" at this event. Our family, our friends, our loved ones whom we desperately want to be included—they all must be "the bride." It may be warfare to help such a thing happen, I know. But that is an unavoidable fact of salvation as it is revealed in Revelation 19 and 20.

And it is an unavoidable challenge. And blessing as well. We who are the bride of Christ can amplify the joy of the feast and get our loved ones there not by hanging around the punch bowl ourselves but by doing all we can to make sure they are also included in the wedding supper of the Lamb.

Prayer

Lord Jesus, I am blessed and sobered by the vision of salvation you revealed to John. Thank you for my salvation. Thank you for coming for me and finding me where I was. Thank you for cleansing me and making me pure. Thank you for making me your own, binding me to you forever, and crushing my past while ensuring my future.

But I know the story goes on. There are still enemies to be subdued and warfare to be waged. Arm me. Steel my nerves. En-courage me, that I may go out and fight evil and indifference and bring fresh new recruits to both wedding and war. Amen.

11

Your Best Life—Soon!

Every story will be written soon;
The blood is on the moon,
Morning will come soon
                    —Josh Garrels

If you are reading this book, there is a very good chance that you are among the wealthiest people in the world.

That may sound crazy to you. You may struggle to pay your bills. You may often go without the things you want. You may drive an old, beat-up car. Your idea of "return on investment" may be finding coins in the couch cushions. You may eat your cereal with a fork so you can use the milk again the next day.

But, believe it or not, measured against the rest of the world, you may be surprised at how well off you are. World Bank economist Branko Milanovic, in his book *The Haves and the Have-Nots* calculates that those earning just $1,225 a year are richer than half the world's population. Those who earn $5,000 a year are in the top 20 percent, worldwide. Those making $12,000 a year? They are the top 10 percent. And an annual income of $34,000 puts you in the top 1 percent of the world's population.[198]

It seems hard to believe. We are richer than we know. Certainly richer than we feel. And that is true not only when we measure against the rest of the world, but also according to the past. When I was growing up in a middle-class Cincinnati, Ohio, suburb, none of the families in my neighborhood owned two cars, and few had a garage. Now, a two-car garage is the minimum for many families, who even then have to park a car or two in the driveway or on the street.

I remember feeling like the poor kid on our block, partly because our refrigerator seldom held more than a bottle of milk, a jug filled with tap water, and a few condiments (ketchup, mustard, etc.). I marveled at the refrigerators in my friends' homes—they had actual food on the shelves. But I probably would have fainted dead away not only at the contents but at the size of most refrigerators today. Compared to my mother's Frigidaire, they look like Apollo rockets.

As a child, I dreamed of a future in which refrigerators were full, homes and cars were air-conditioned, television shows were in color, and the cuffs of my pants reached all the way to the tops of my shoes. And those dreams have been more than fulfilled. More than exceeded, in fact (unfortunately, it's the *waist* of my pants that worry me these days, not the cuffs. But even that is an indicator of how good I've got it).

But as far beyond my wildest dreams as my comforts and advantages are today, they cannot even begin to compare with what awaits me. And you. And all who have experienced new life through faith in Jesus Christ.

Your Best Life Isn't Now

In 2004, the television preacher and pastor of Lakewood Church in Houston, Texas, published his first book, entitled *Your Best Life Now!* The book—did I mention it was his first?—has since sold roughly a bajillion copies.

With all due respect, I think Pastor Joel's book title is all wrong. I get what he's saying, but the truth of the matter is, your best life isn't now. Your best life is yet to come. Even if you're not suffering persecution as the first-century readers and hearers of The Revelation were. Even if you're not going through hard times. Even if your refrigerator is the size of an Apollo rocket and your pants reach all the way to the tops of your shoes. Your best life isn't now. But it will be soon.

The Revelation of Jesus Christ to John, his beloved disciple, reveals one wonder after another through the first twenty chapters. It reveals a glorified Jesus as the Lamb on the throne, worthy of the greatest praise heaven can offer, yet still willing to condescend to touch those who encounter him. It reveals his intense and intimate concern for even the smallest and weakest of churches. It reveals the importance and impact of worship on heaven and on earth—and on you and me. It reveals the reality of evil in this world even as it shows the sure victory of the church. It reveals the absolute necessity of prayer, especially in light of the circumstances that surround us. It reveals the power of witness in the last days. It reveals critical perspectives on history, politics, and religion. It reveals the certainty of the judgment that is to come and the glorious salvation that belongs to all who have placed their trust in Christ.

Through all that, the message of The Revelation is one of hope and blessing. It doesn't ignore evil and the tragic events that surround us and are yet to come upon us, but it nonetheless unfolds a great cosmic story of victory and glory. But the first twenty chapters of The Revelation are in some respects like my dreams of full refrigerators and pants that fit. They are prelude to something far more wonderful than the reader or the hearer can conceive, for chapter 21 opens to a new vision of that which will be: your best life—soon.

The New Life

What's the most sudden and drastic change you've ever experienced?

I was on a plane some years ago, traveling from my home in Ohio to Dallas. The boarding process had proceeded flawlessly, and the plane left the gate right on time. Everything was going according to schedule. Everything was running smoothly. Once in the air, the plane leveled out at our cruising altitude, and the flight attendants began serving drinks and snacks to the passengers. The pilot had no sooner come onto the speaker system to suggest that the flight attendants take their seats due to some turbulence ahead, when it suddenly felt like the plane dropped from the sky. I don't know if we dropped a hundred feet or a thousand, but I think more people would have screamed if their stomachs hadn't been lodged in their throats. Somehow, the flight attendants managed to hold on and in just a few seconds, the crisis had passed. The rest of the flight passed without incident, but I'm pretty sure that fairly important parts of my body had to be scraped off the ceiling of the aircraft that day.

There is a shift from chapter 20 of The Revelation to chapter 21 that rivals that flight. In chapter 20, John describes an angel coming down from heaven and tossing the devil, Satan, into the abyss to be imprisoned there for a thousand years. Next, chapter 20 describes the release of Satan from that prison, only to be defeated one last time and thrown into the lake of fire. Then, death itself and Hell itself are cast into the lake of fire, along with the poor souls whose names were not written in the Lamb's Book of Life.

With that, chapter 21 opens:

> Then I saw "a new heaven and a new earth," for the first heaven and the first earth had passed away, and there was no longer any sea.[199]

Contrary to how most of us picture "heaven," John sees a thoroughly physical representation of eternity. He does not see angels floating on gossamer clouds (whatever "gossamer" is). He does not hear the music of harps and choirs. He sees a fresh new heaven and earth, free of all the tragedy and danger of the first heaven and the first earth (represented by the absence of a sea).

> I saw the Holy City, the new Jerusalem, coming down out of heaven from God, prepared as a bride beautifully dressed for her husband. And I heard a loud voice from the throne saying, "Look! God's dwelling place is now among the people, and he will dwell with them. They will be his people, and God himself will be with them and be their God. 'He will wipe every tear from their eyes. There will be no more death' or mourning or crying or pain, for the old order of things has passed away."
>
> He who was seated on the throne said, "I am mak-

ing everything new!" Then he said, "Write this down, for these words are trustworthy and true."[200]

Most startling of all, *you* appeared in John's vision of this new heaven and new earth. When he sees the Holy City, the new Jerusalem, appearing as a bride on her wedding day, he recognizes the church, the bride of Christ, you and me, as a loud voice announces that the prophecy of Ezekiel has been completely and finally fulfilled:

> My dwelling place shall be with them, and I will be their God, and they shall be my people.[201]

Your best life is coming soon—a life that is the glorious fulfillment of all the "best" things you've experienced so far. Has the power of Jesus Christ made you clean? You will be cleaner still. Has the Lord made beautiful things out of the brokenness you offered to him? You will be more beautiful still. Have you experienced the sweetness of his smile, the comfort of his presence, the healing power of his touch? Your best life will be all that and more—soon.

Whatever joy and beauty you have experienced as a result of your relationship with God in Christ—as lovely as it is—he will make it new.

The Rich Life

In May of 2009, my wife and I traveled to Peru. After seven or eight days among the beautiful people of Arequipa, Peru's second largest city, we journeyed to Cusco and then on to Machu Picchu, one of the wonders of the world.

Machu Picchu is located on a mountaintop in the Andes. It was built in the 1400s, at the height of the Incan Empire, and was inhabited by a few hundred people for just over one hundred years. In 1911, though the locals had long known of its existence, Machu Picchu was "discovered" by American historian Hiram Bingham.

To get to the site, we crawled into a cab around 4 A.M. and endured a breakneck ninety-minute drive to a train station. Arriving just as the train was leaving, we paid the driver and made a mad dash for the train, making it just in time. After a couple hours on the train, we transferred to a bus, which snaked up the side of a mountain to the visitor's center at Machu Picchu. But when we got there, we weren't there. Yet.

We climbed a tall and demanding series of steps before we got our first sight of Machu Picchu. And, while we carried ample water supplies from the start of our journey, our water ran out soon after we started climbing. We took our time. We shed our jackets. But nothing could compensate for the lack of fresh, cold, clean water.

Maybe you've traveled in places where clean water is a rarity. If not, you'll have to take my word for it: clean, fresh, cool water is irreplaceable. Having it makes you rich. The lack of it makes you poor. This was especially so in the first-century places familiar to John and the first readers and hearers of The Revelation.

> He said to me: "It is done. I am the Alpha and the Omega, the Beginning and the End. To the thirsty I will give water without cost from the spring of the water of life. Those who are victorious will inherit all this, and I will be their God and they will be my children. But the cowardly, the unbelieving, the vile, the murderers, the sexually immoral, those who practice magic arts, the idolaters and all liars— they will be consigned to the fiery lake of burning sulfur. This is the second death."[202]

The image Jesus uses to communicate the rich life to John and his readers is "water without cost from the spring of the water of life." It is not the image a modern writer might have used—unless he had climbed to Machu Picchu with an inadequate supply of drinking water. But the image is this: the most valuable commodity will be yours, free of charge, in abundance, by right of inheritance. And the implication is, if you can have "water without cost from the spring of the water of life," you can have anything. You are rich. But the wealth and happiness of your best life extends even further.

It may be jarring, after all the beauty, comfort, and newness of Revelation 21:1–7, to read verse 8, about those who will be consigned to the lake of fire. But I don't think the point of those words about the "cowardly, the unbelieving, the vile, the murderers, the sexually immoral" and so on is mean-spirited or vengeful at all. I think the point is that none of those behaviors or experiences will be around any longer, to spoil your best life. Verse 8 is a promise, too, though it is stated in the negative. The promise is that sinful, negative, destructive behavior will be eternally absent from the life that awaits you.

The Beautiful Life

Even the most glittering of earthly lives has its share of sorrow and pain. Steve Jobs, one of the wealthiest men on earth, could not buy the bodily health that would have prolonged his life beyond the age of fifty-six. Queen Elizabeth II, despite a long and honorable reign as queen of England, suffered numerous griefs and disappointments in her family over the years. Many of the most gorgeous Hollywood stars seem unable to find and nurture a love that will survive temptation and last forever.

But Revelation 21 promises that it will not be so with you. Your future's so bright, the angels will have to wear shades.

> One of the seven angels who had the seven bowls full of the seven last plagues came and said to me, "Come, I will show you the bride, the wife of the Lamb." And he carried me away in the Spirit to a mountain great and high, and showed me the Holy City, Jerusalem, coming down out of heaven from God. It shone with the glory of God, and its brilliance was like that of a very precious jewel,

like a jasper, clear as crystal. It had a great, high wall with
twelve gates, and with twelve angels at the gates. On the
gates were written the names of the twelve tribes of Israel.
There were three gates on the east, three on the north,
three on the south and three on the west. The wall of the
city had twelve foundations, and on them were the names
of the twelve apostles of the Lamb.[203]

Those few verses, in which the angel shows John the bride of Christ—
which includes you and me, and all who have experienced new life in
Christ—feature several symbolic characteristics:

You are beautiful. The Holy City, the new Jerusalem, is described as
shining with the glory of God and brilliant like a glistening jewel. That
is a description of your new reality, your best life. However you feel
now about your life, your physical appearance, your personality, and
so forth, no words will be adequate to describe your beauty in eternity.
You "will shine brilliantly, like the cloudless, star-strewn night skies."[204]

You are secure. The city the angel shows John has "a great, high
wall with twelve gates"—three on each side—"and with twelve angels at the gates." Your fast-approaching reality and reward will be a
life free from threat, danger, and discomfort. There will be no chance
of abuse. No possibility of mistreatment. Nothing to fear.

You are accepted. John's vision of your future state reveals the
names of the twelve tribes of Israel on the gates and the names of
the twelve apostles on the foundation stones. In other words, you
are accepted and prized no less than Judah, Reuben, Benjamin, or
Dan. You don't have to strive for acceptance, you don't have to win
approval; you are accepted right alongside Peter, James, John, and
Andrew. Your best life is one of total and eternal acceptance.

The Expansive Life

The next thing to happen in John's vision is an echo of something
that happened in the vision of Ezekiel, nearly seven hundred years

earlier. In Ezekiel's vision, at a moment in history when the holy city of Jerusalem was in ruins and God's people had been dragged into long, hard captivity in a foreign land, Ezekiel said that God took him to the land of Israel and perched him on "a very high mountain."[205] There, he was shown a vision of a walled city, Jerusalem, carefully measured and beautifully restored, to indicate that God would redeem his people, and that a glorious future still lay before them.

John the Apostle's audience in the late first century would have been thoroughly familiar with Ezekiel's vision and what it represented as they read or heard what happens next:

> The angel who talked with me had a measuring rod of gold to measure the city, its gates and its walls. The city was laid out like a square, as long as it was wide. He measured the city with the rod and found it to be 12,000 stadia in length, and as wide and high as it is long. The angel measured the wall using human measurement, and it was 144 cubits thick. The wall was made of jasper, and the city of pure gold, as pure as glass. The foundations of the city walls were decorated with every kind of precious stone. The first foundation was jasper, the second sapphire, the third agate, the fourth emerald, the fifth onyx, the sixth ruby, the seventh chrysolite, the eighth beryl, the ninth topaz, the tenth turquoise, the eleventh jacinth, and the twelfth amethyst. The twelve gates were twelve pearls, each gate made of a single pearl. The great street of the city was of gold, as pure as transparent glass.
>
> I did not see a temple in the city, because the Lord God Almighty and the Lamb are its temple. The city does not need the sun or the moon to shine on it, for the glory of God gives it light, and the Lamb is its lamp. The nations will walk by its light, and the kings of the earth will bring their splendor into it. On no day will its gates ever

be shut, for there will be no night there. The glory and honor of the nations will be brought into it. Nothing impure will ever enter it, nor will anyone who does what is shameful or deceitful, but only those whose names are written in the Lamb's book of life.[206]

No one in John's first audience would have missed the significance of that scene, and neither should we. It describes a future for the church—the bride of Christ—that is bigger than anything we have experienced to date. Earl F. Palmer, pastor emeritus of University Presbyterian Church in Seattle, in his commentary on The Revelation, points out the immensity of the dimensions John describes:

> It [the city] is a perfect cube, twelve thousand stadia in length, height, and width. This means, in terms of miles, that the city is 1500 miles in each direction. Even in an era of supersonic speeds, this is a city that takes our breath away.[207]

Years ago, I was driving my family from our Ohio home to a vacation spot in Maine. On the way, we stayed overnight with some friends in lower Manhattan. When we resumed our journey, I deduced from the map that the most direct route to take would be a path straight up the middle of that island until we reached I-95, which would then become the New England Thruway. On paper, it looked like a reasonable plan.

I had been to New York many times but obviously had no grasp of the scale of the city. Block after block, neighborhood after neighborhood, it went on and on. And on. There seemed to be no end to it, or to the traffic we encountered on the way. We finally made it, but not before I gained a new appreciation for the dimensions of that great city.

The city John describes in The Revelation dwarfs every earthly city in man's experience. It is intended to show us—not only by its size but also by its wealth, brightness, activity, and purity—what our destiny is. Your "best life"—which is coming, and coming soon—

will be bigger and better than you can dream. It will dazzle you. It will take your breath away. And it will never end.

The Whole Life

There are many misconceptions—even among Christians—about the life to come: that we will be angels and have wings and play harps, for example. (Angels are angels, and people are people; what's so hard to keep straight?) Another common misconception is that we will float on fluffy clouds and have nothing to do. That doesn't sound appealing at all to me. Especially if my cloud is more than ten feet off the ground.

Your best life will not be that of a couch potato, or even a cloud potato. The Revelation makes that clear in chapter 22, verses 1–5:

> Then the angel showed me the river of the water of life, as clear as crystal, flowing from the throne of God and of the Lamb down the middle of the great street of the city. On each side of the river stood the tree of life, bearing twelve crops of fruit, yielding its fruit every month. And the leaves of the tree are for the healing of the nations. No longer will there be any curse. The throne of God and of the Lamb will be in the city, and his servants will serve him. They will see his face, and his name will be on their foreheads. There will be no more night. They will not need the light of a lamp or the light of the sun, for the Lord God will give them light. And they will reign for ever and ever.[208]

According to those verses, the life that is to come for you will be characterized by all the things we most long for but that are elusive or unattainable in this life because of the fall, because of sin:

1. *Wholeness.* The sight of the river of life and the tree of life in the city indicate a return to the Garden, that

state in which humans were created, when everything was good. Revelation 22 clearly depicts the complete and lasting reversal of Genesis 3. Not only does the river flow and the tree bear fruit but the leaves of the tree heal the nations. Everyone will be whole again. There will be no curse. There will be no sin. No devil. No disease. No infirmity. No limitation.

2. *Intimacy*. All the obstacles and impediments to your relationship with God will be gone in the life that is to come. God will be with you, and in you, in more intimate ways than you have yet experienced. You will see him "face to face,"[209] as Paul the apostle put it. You will never lose sight of him, and when you look in the mirror you will see his name written all over you, claiming you as his own.

3. *Freedom*. For the ancients—as for many in our day and age—night was a dangerous time. There were no streetlamps or security lights to make things safer after nightfall. Night was the time to head for home, close the shutters, lock the doors, and wait for the safety that would come with morning light. Even now, there are some things you cannot do or places you should not go after dark. But your best life—the one that is to come—will be different. "There will never be night again,"[210] because the blazing presence of God will be in you and all around you. You will enjoy a freedom no human being has ever experienced.

4. *Employment*. The conventional idea of the next life would have us believe that we will enjoy lives of unceasing leisure and relaxation. But that is not what John's vision says. The Revelation says that you will have dual roles in the new Jerusalem: servant and king (or queen). You will serve him, in ways you can only dream of now. If the songs

you write or sing now are imperfect, they will be infinitely better then. If the meals you create in this life sometimes flop, every one will be an award winner then. If the homes you build today are the best you can do with the time and budget you have, they will be dream-homes-come-true to you then. There will be differences, of course. In the next life, you will not labor for money. You will not work for man. You will serve your gracious God and Father and the Lamb who sits on the throne. You will do the things you may only have dreamed of in this life.

But verse 5 says you will also *reign* forever and ever. Your service to God will include reigning, ruling, acting as coregent with God. Tim Lahaye, in his book *Revelation Unveiled*, comments, "Whether that will involve universes, galaxies, and other planets can only be guessed at. But one thing is for certain: We will reign with Him forever."[211]

You are not living your best life now. You've begun it, if you have experienced new life in Christ, but you have so much more—so much better—to look forward to. In fact, the Apostle Paul suggested that, however hard your life may be at this moment, your present troubles will be far outweighed by your best life—soon.[212] So hang on. Your best life—new, rich, beautiful, expansive, and whole—is coming soon.

Prayer

Gracious Father, thank you for all I have to look forward to that is mine by grace through faith in Jesus Christ. Lift my gaze from the mundane, often gritty, details of my life right now to the best life—new, rich, beautiful, expansive, and whole—that awaits me. Help me to live now so as to prepare for my life—soon, in Jesus' name, amen.

12

Your Last Words

Yea, Amen! let all adore Thee,
High on Thine eternal throne;
Savior, take the power and glory,
Claim the kingdom for Thine own;
O come quickly! O come quickly! O come quickly!
Everlasting God, come down!

—Charles Wesley

Lady Astor was the first female member of the British parliament. On her deathbed, she awoke and saw herself surrounded by family members. Her last words? "Am I dying? Or is this my birthday?"

Ethan Allen—the American patriot, not the furniture store—was told by his doctor, "General, I am afraid the angels are waiting for you," to which Allen replied, "Waiting are they? Waiting are they? Well, let 'em wait!"

The dying words of Pancho Villa, the famous Mexican bandit, were, "Don't let it end like this. Tell them I said something."

And General John Sedgwick, a Union commander at the Battle of Spotsylvania uttered the famous last words, "They couldn't hit an elephant at this dista—"

If you were given a chance to plan your last words, what would they be? If you knew the next thing you spoke would be it, what would you say?

Please don't let it be a rhetorical question. Take a minute. Think about it. Maybe even scrawl an idea or two in the margin of this book. What would your last words be?

The Final Words in the Bible

My wife has claimed more than once that her last words are likely to be, "Bob! Do you see that stop sign?" Which means that my last words may well be, "What stop sign?"

It's not an idle question. I hope you've given it some thought, as it forms a fitting preparation for the final chapter in this book on final things. If you've stuck with me this far, I hope that means you've enjoyed—and been blessed by—this journey through the most enigmatic book of the Bible. I know I have. It has truly been a joy for me, as a Bible student *and* as a writer, as a follower of Jesus *and* as a fellow traveler with you.

I hope it has been—for you—a fresh and living and intensely practical look at this revelation that is so often used to confuse or scare or steer people away from the central business of life, which is *to know God and make him known.*

And it's not over yet. Because we have yet to confront what may be (according to the collected wisdom and testimony of the ancient church, at least) the very last written words of God to men, the final words entrusted to an apostle, the last words of the 775,000 words in the Bible, and, in terms of when they were recorded, in perhaps the last decade of the first century, the very last Biblical words to be recorded.

Seems like a pretty big deal to me. It may be something we should pay close attention to.

So let's have a look at the last words of Revelation 22. The last words of The Revelation. The last words of the whole Bible, as revealed by Jesus himself to his close friend and follower John. Here they are. Read them carefully. Slowly. Give them the consideration that is due to the last words of God to man:

> The angel said to me, "These words are trustworthy and true. The Lord, the God of the spirits of the prophets, sent his angel to show his servants the things that must soon take place."
>
> "Behold, I am coming soon! Blessed is he who keeps the words of the prophecy in this book."
>
> I, John, am the one who heard and saw these things. And when I had heard and seen them, I fell down to worship at the feet of the angel who had been showing them to me. But he said to me, "Do not do it! I am a fellow ser-

vant with you and with your brothers the prophets and of all who keep the words of this book. Worship God!"

Then he told me, "Do not seal up the words of the prophecy of this book, because the time is near. Let him who does wrong continue to do wrong; let him who is vile continue to be vile; let him who does right continue to do right; and let him who is holy continue to be holy."

"Behold, I am coming soon! My reward is with me, and I will give to everyone according to what he has done. I am the Alpha and the Omega, the First and the Last, the Beginning and the End.

"Blessed are those who wash their robes, that they may have the right to the tree of life and may go through the gates into the city. Outside are the dogs, those who practice magic arts, the sexually immoral, the murderers, the idolaters and everyone who loves and practices falsehood.

"I, Jesus, have sent my angel to give you this testimony for the churches. I am the Root and the Offspring of David, and the bright Morning Star."

The Spirit and the bride say, "Come!" And let him who hears say, "Come!" Whoever is thirsty, let him come; and whoever wishes, let him take the free gift of the water of life.

I warn everyone who hears the words of the prophecy of this book: If anyone adds anything to them, God will add to him the plagues described in this book. And if anyone takes words away from this book of prophecy, God will take away from him his share in the tree of life and in the holy city, which are described in this book.

He who testifies to these things says, "Yes, I am coming soon."

Amen. Come, Lord Jesus.

The grace of the Lord Jesus be with God's people. Amen.[213]

Do you remember how this revelation started out? Do you recall the introduction to John's record of this extraordinary vision? It began with these words from chapter 1:

> The revelation of Jesus Christ, which God gave him to show his servants what must soon take place. He made it known by sending his angel to his servant John, who testifies to everything he saw—that is, the word of God and the testimony of Jesus Christ. Blessed is the one who reads the words of this prophecy, and blessed are those who hear it and take to heart what is written in it, because the time is near.[214]

The very first words of this book promise not only to reveal coming events but also to bless "the one who reads" and "those who hear it and take to heart what is written in it." It is intended to bless you. Not to scare you. Not to confuse you. Not to whip you into line. But to bless you . . . if you take it to heart.

That is what we were told at the beginning of The Revelation. And it is what we are told at the end, in words spoken by Jesus himself:

> "Blessed is he who keeps the words of the prophecy in this book."[215]

It is a book of blessing.

We are blessed to have it. We are blessed to read it, hear it, and heed it. We are blessed to keep it, to keep coming back to it, to obey its commands and lessons and reminders and challenges.

Please keep that in mind—that the path to blessing is the way of obedience. That is what is meant by *keeping* the words of the prophecy of this book. It doesn't just mean holding onto them, retaining possession of them in your bookcase or on your bedside table. It means hewing to them. Observing them. Obeying them. Making them a part of your life.

If the intended blessing of The Revelation is to be truly and fully felt by you, in your life, there is one final key: "[keep] the words of the prophecy in this book."[216] That seems like a lot, doesn't it? There are roughly twelve thousand words (depending on the translation) in the book of Revelation. So it would be a daunting task to heed them all. But fear not. Be blessed. I think chapter 22 boils it down for you, and for me, to three obedient acts, three ways to keep the prophecy of this book, the main thrust of these "last words" in this last book of the Bible.

Worship

Notice what happens in verses 8 and 9 of Revelation's last chapter:

> I, John, am the one who heard and saw these things. And when I had heard and seen them, I fell down to worship at the feet of the angel who had been showing them to me. But he said to me, "Do not do it! I am a fellow servant with you and with your brothers the prophets and of all who keep the words of this book. Worship God!"[217]

This is the *second* time John has fallen down to worship the angel. He did it in chapter 19, too. And now he does it again.

What is his problem? If anyone ought to know better, John should, right?

After all, he is Jesus' Beloved Disciple. He walked the streets of Jerusalem with Jesus. He sailed the Sea of Galilee in Jesus' company. He saw Jesus transfigured. He saw him alive after his resurrection.

He saw him ascend to heaven. How could John, of all people, make such a mistake, not once, but twice?

I think it's for the same reason we do.

Eugene Peterson, whom I have quoted often because he inspired the perspective and the approach for this book, writes this:

> It is easier. It is easier to indulge in ecstasies than to engage in obedience. It is easier to pursue a fascination with the supernatural than to enter into the service of God. And because it is easier, it happens more often. . . . Revealing angels have always proved more popular than the revealed God.[218]

I've seen it. Maybe you have, too. I've been in worship settings and prayer meetings in which all the talk afterward is about angels being seen or felt. I confess I'm often jealous of those who report such sightings and sensations, particularly since some of them are people I thoroughly trust and respect. But, while I have had many utterly rapturous worship experiences, in private and in corporate worship, I suspect that my Father knows my temptation would be to indulge in ecstasies rather than to engage in obedience. I would be too quick to bow to angels.

Maybe we all are, as John was. But the angel wastes no time. He stops John cold.

He says, "Don't do it. . . . Worship God."

I believe the angel's message to John is intended also for us.

Worship God.

Time and time again through The Revelation, we have been shown a vision of worship. Over and over we have been called up— with John—into the very worship of heaven.

Worship is central to this book, and it ought to be central to my life as well.

I know that there are some around us who "attend" church, who "catch" a worship service when it's convenient for them, who figure they're doing great if they average about every other week, and who don't understand why some people actually talk about worshiping at home, every day, sometimes a couple times a day or throughout the day.

They don't get it.

And neither do they get the blessing this book promises.

"Blessed is he who keeps the words of the prophecy in this book."[219]

Rory Noland, in his book *Worship on Earth as It Is in Heaven*, writes,

> Thanks to the vivid firsthand accounts from John . . . we can close our eyes whenever we want and picture worship in heaven: the magnificent colors, the glorious voices, the bright light. Those stunningly intriguing four living creatures and the elders clothed in pure white falling down before the Lamb. Myriads of angels and that great multitude, stretched out as far as the eye can see, from every nation, tribe, and tongue—all with faces to the ground. The sheer beauty of it all takes my breath away.
>
> Sometimes as I'm poring over a psalm and my heart is stirred by a certain attribute of God, I remember that at that very moment, worship in heaven is in full swing. It happens at church too. While singing along with God's people, I'll realize that the most glorious worship of all is resounding throughout heaven at the same time. In those moments, I sense the Lord inviting me to do more than just gaze heavenward. God is inviting me to join in heaven's worship, to add my voice to the celestial choir. In

fact, Ephesians 2:6 states that, because of Christ, we are already "seated . . . in the heavenly places."

So let's worship as if we're already there. Let's worship God with a mighty voice as if we're already with him in paradise.[220]

Worship God.

Make worship central to your life.

Make worshiping God the focus of your life . . . and you will be blessed.

Watch

Three times in the last fifteen verses of The Revelation, we hear the voice of Jesus saying, "I am coming soon."[221]

Don't just take my word for it. Look it up in your Bible. Circle that phrase.

Verse 7, "Behold, I am coming soon."

Verse 12, "Behold, I am coming soon."

Verse 20, "Yes, I am coming soon."

When he was on earth, Jesus promised,

> "In the future you will see the Son of Man . . . coming on the clouds of heaven."[222]

And he had told his followers, "Take heed, watch."[223]

In the Gospel that bears his name, John himself had recorded Jesus' words:

> "If I go and prepare a place for you, I will come again and receive you unto myself."[224]

And The Revelation had begun with the announcement,

Look, he is coming with the clouds,
and every eye will see him.[225]

The Lord went on to say it twice more in this revelation, in chapter 3:

I am coming soon.[226]

And in chapter 16:

Behold, I come like a thief! Blessed is he who stays
awake.[227]

Earl Palmer points out in his commentary on The Revelation how
Aleksander Solzhenitsyn, in his short novel *One Day in the Life of
Ivan Denisovich*, described the character, Alyoska:

Alyoska, the young Christian, is in the same bunkhouse
with the rest of the prisoners; he has the same ten-year
sentence as the rest; he works on the same work crew, but
he "reads his Gospels facing the light bulb."[228]

Alyoska is in the same predicament as all the others. He is as mis-
treated as the others. He is no more likely to survive the camp than
the others. But he "reads his Gospels facing the light bulb."

He has a hope. A future. He faces the light. He lives in expectation.

And so must I. So must you. So, in Jesus' name, I urge you:
watch.

Look for the glorious appearing of our Lord and Savior Jesus
Christ. Expect him. Live in expectation. Pray in expectation. Order
your life around this reality. Schedule your time around it.

Take heed . . . watch . . . and you will be blessed.

Come

The book of The Revelation and its twenty-second chapter are all about the soon coming of Jesus. But it's also about a *second* coming.

Jesus says repeatedly in Revelation 22, "I am coming soon." But if you look again at verse 17, you'll see:

> The Spirit and the bride say, "Come!" And let him who hears say, "Come!"[229]

The Spirit, of course, is the Holy Spirit of God, the second person of the Trinity, the threefold person of God. When Jesus says, "I'm coming soon," the Holy Spirit says, "Come!"

The "bride" referred to in that verse is the bride of Christ, the church—all who have been forgiven and cleansed and born again by grace through faith. When Jesus says, "I'm coming soon," the church, too, says "Come!"

And then verse 17 says, "And let him who hears say, 'Come!'" Those are directed to the people who first heard these words read aloud in their gathering time as a church. And to all those since. And to me. And you.

In other words, everyone's on board. In heaven and on earth, all are agreed. From history long past to this present day, the plea reaches heaven: Come, Lord Jesus!

Come into our world.

Come and make all things right.

Come on the clouds, let every eye see you, let the whole world be filled with your glory as the waters cover the sea.

But there is a second coming in that verse. Not the "Second Coming," capital S, capital C. But a second coming that is urged in Revelation 22:

Whoever is thirsty, let him come; and whoever wishes, let him take the free gift of the water of life.[230]

Because, you see, there are still those who, when the Spirit says, "Come," they say, "No!"

There are still those who, when the church says, "Come," they say, "Not yet!"

There are those who, when others around them cry, "Come," they say, "Wait!"

But Jesus says, "I am coming soon." In no uncertain terms, "I am coming soon." Whatever anyone may say, "I am coming soon."

So he also says, in this revelation,

Is anyone thirsty? Come!
All who will, come and drink,
Drink freely of the Water of Life![231]

Come, he says. Come without pretense, without pride, without condition, without delay.

These are the last words of God to you. They are the last words of Jesus' heart to your heart. He says, "Come."

If you have not yet come to him in humility and repentance to ask for the forgiveness of your sins and the salvation of your soul, then his "Come" is urging you to read no further—to do nothing else—until you heed his loving appeal (turn to p. xxx for a suggested prayer to help you).

If you have strayed from him and have turned away from him, the spring of living water, to try to satisfy your soul's thirst with wells you have dug yourself, then he bids you to "come" and once more "pull up buckets of water / from the wells of salvation."[232]

If you are struggling to live in these last days under your own power, in your own strength, then hear his "come" as a heartfelt plea to throw yourself on him and experience his all-sufficient grace, power, love, and mercy.

If you're weighed down by care, exhausted by effort, discouraged by circumstances, or feeling betrayed or abandoned by friends, hear him say, "Come." He is the answer to your heart's questions, the fulfillment of your life's need. Now and always, moment by moment, he says, "Come.

Please don't let your last words to him be, "Later."

Or, "not now."

Or, "I don't know."

Whatever your situation, whatever your need, don't let your answer to his final, fervent, and recurring word be anything but "Yes."

Yes, Lord. Come.

Prayer

Come, Lord Jesus. Come to my heart right now. Come to my life. Come to my family. Come to my church, to my workplace. Come to my friends and neighbors. Come to my community and to my nation. Come to this world.

Come to the thirsty. Come to the desperate. To the sad and sorrowing. To the hurting and hungry. To the sick and to the lonely. Come, Lord.

Come and make all things right. Come soon. Come on the clouds, let every eye see you, let the whole world be filled with your glory, as the waters cover the sea. Amen. Come, Lord Jesus.

Appendix

A Prayer of Surrender and Commitment

There is no one-size-fits-all prayer for becoming a follower of Jesus Christ. We are not told with what words Peter, Matthew, and others among Jesus' first followers responded to his call to "follow me." They may have said, simply, "Yes." But we do know that they left everything else and became his *talmudim* (students and companions) as he taught multitudes, healed the sick, and even raised the dead. They saw what he was doing. They enlisted in what he was doing. Eventually, they began to do the things he was doing.[233]

Following Jesus today is not a matter of saying a prayer and then going about your daily life as you always did. However your journey begins, it must be followed by a prayerful, trusting, daily intention to follow Jesus, to see what he is doing, enlist in what he is doing, and participate in what he is doing.

I have known some people to begin following Jesus with a simple "yes" or "here I am." I have known some who expressed their surrender and commitment with the help of a hymn or a printed prayer. But, in every case, the thoughts and sentiments in the following prayer were present, whether they were expressed verbally or not.

Feel free to use this prayer as a guide, adapting it and expanding it as the spirit of God leads you. There is no power in the prayer itself; the power is in the sincerity and faith with which you repent, surrender, and commit your life to the Lord Jesus Christ:

Lord Jesus, I come to you like every other human being,
as a sinner in need of your mercy and forgiveness.
Lord, have mercy on me, a sinner.
Thank you for coming to this earth,
living as a human being just like me,
dying a cruel and painful death as a sacrifice for my sins,
and rising from the dead to defeat the power of sin, death,
and hell.
I renounce my sins and my former way of life,
and, on the basis of your sacrifice on the cross,
I ask you to forgive all my sins,
cleanse me from them,
and deliver me from their power.
Come into my heart, Lord Jesus.
I give you my life, surrender to your control, and submit to
your Lordship,
asking you to lead me by your Holy Spirit
and teach me day by day to trust you and follow you,
to see what you are doing, enlist in what you are doing, and
participate in it,
with your help,
amen.

Notes

1. Robert Frost. "Fire and Ice," *The Poetry of Robert Frost* (New York: Holt, Rinehart and Winston, 1969), 220.
2. Eliot, T. S., ed. Jough Dempsey, "The Hollow Men," *Poetry X* (13 Jul 2003).
3. http://www.teenhelp.org/forums/f39-religion-spirituality-science-philosophy/t20067-help-fear-end-world/.
4. See comment, http://www.everydayhealth.com/forums/anxiety-disorders/topic/overwhelming-fear-about-end-of-the-world.
5. "Mass suicide warning as French fears rise," *Herald Sun*, June 16, 2011.
6. Maia de la Baume, "For End of the World, a French Peak Holds Allure," *The New York Times*, January 30, 2011.
7. John 20:31.
8. 1 John 5:13.
9. Revelation 1:1.
10. *In the Twinkling of an Eye* (New York: Fleming H. Revell Company, 1933) and *The Mark of the Beast* (New York: Fleming H. Revell Company, 1933).
11. Revelation 1:1–3.
12. Revelation 1:3.
13. 1 Thessalonians 4:18.
14. Revelation 1:4–16.
15. Revelation 1:12.
16. Revelation 1:17–20.
17. Revelation 1:17b.
18. Revelation 1:1–4a, 9–11 EVS.
19. Eugene Peterson, *Reversed Thunder* (New York: HarperCollins, 1988), 47.
20. Revelation 1:1.
21. Revelation 2:1b.

22. Revelation 2:8b.
23. Revelation 2:12b.
24. Revelation 2:18b.
25. Revelation 3:1b.
26. Revelation 3:7b.
27. Revelation 3:14b.
28. Revelation 2:2.
29. Matthew 24:24.
30. 1 John 4:1.
31. Revelation 2:3.
32. Revelation 2:4–5.
33. The letter identified in our Bibles as "Ephesians" may have been intended as a circular letter to virtually the same churches Jesus addresses in Revelation 2 and 3, but the Ephesian church would have been among those churches, in any case.
34. Ephesians 1:15–16.
35. Revelation 2:9–10.
36. J. Ramsey Michaels, *IVP New Testament Commentary: Revelation* (Downers Grove, IL: InterVarsity Press, 1997), 72.
37. Revelation 2:13.
38. Revelation 2:14–16.
39. Acts 15:20.
40. http://teotwawkiblog.blogspot.com/.
41. Revelation 2:19.
42. Revelation 2:20–23.
43. Romans 12:9.
44. Revelation 3:1–3.
45. Revelation 3:8.
46. Revelation 3:10.
47. Revelation 3:15–16.
48. Revelation 3:17.
49. John R. W. Stott, *What Christ Thinks of the Church* (Wheaton: Harold Shaw, 1990), 116.
50. Revelation 3:19.
51. Revelation 3:19 KJV.
52. Revelation 3:19 HCSB.
53. Revelation 3:19 NLT.
54. Revelation 3:19, Amplified Bible (emphasis in original).
55. Revelation 3:20.
56. Brennan Manning, *The Ragamuffin Gospel* (Sisters, OR: Multnomah, 2005), 59.
57. Revelation 2:7b.
58. Revelation 12:1 KJV.
59. Genesis 49:10.
60. Revelation 1:1, 3.
61. Revelation 4:1–3.
62. Revelation 4:3.
63. Revelation 4:4.
64. Revelation 4:5a.

65. Revelation 4:5b.
66. Revelation 4:6a.
67. Revelation 4:6b.
68. Revelation 4:10.
69. Revelation 5:6a.
70. Revelation 5:11a.
71. Revelation 4:4–8.
72. Ezekiel 1:4–10.
73. Revelation 5:11.
74. Revelation 4:9–11.
75. Matthew 5:23–24.
76. Revelation 5:1–10.
77. John 1:1.
78. Revelation 5:11–14.
79. Revelation 5:12.
80. Revelation 5:13b.
81. Revelation 1:1, 3.
82. See, for example, Lerry Fogle, *Revelation Explained* (Plainfield, NJ: Logos International, 1981), 130–131.
83. See, for example, Gail R. O'Day and David L. Petersen, *Theological Bible Commentary* (Louisville, KY: Westminster John Knox, 2009), 475.
84. See, for example, Tim Lahaye, *Revelation Unveiled* (Grand Rapids: Zondervan , 1999), 138–139.
85. Revelation 1:1, 3.
86. Revelation 6:1a.
87. Revelation 6:1b–2.
88. Revelation 6:3–4 NIV.
89. Matthew 24:4–13 NIV.
90. Matthew 24:4–13.
91. Revelation 6:5–6 NIV.
92. Matthew 24:7.
93. Revelation 6:7–8.
94. J. B. Phillips, *The New Testament in Modern English* (New York: MacMillan Publishing Company, 1976), 525.
95. Revelation 6:9–11 NIV.
96. Acts 5:41.
97. Revelation 6:12–17 NIV.
98. Revelation 6:16 NIV.
99. Revelation 6:17 NIV.
100. Revelation 1:1, 3.
101. 1 John 5:18 NIV.
102. Psalm 91:7.
103. Revelation 7:1–8.
104. Ezekiel 9:3–4.
105. 1 John 5:8
106. Revelation 7:9a NIV.

107. Acts 2:9–11.
108. 1 John 5:8.
109. Revelation 7:9b.
110. Revelation 3:4.
111. William Pearson, "Jesus, Thy Fulness Give," *The Song Book of The Salvation Army* (New York: The Salvation Army Supplies, Printing and Publishing Department, 1967), 105.
112. Revelation 7:9c.
113. Romans 8:37.
114. Eugene Peterson, *Reversed Thunder* (New York: HarperCollins, 1988), 85.
115. Revelation 7:10–17 NIV.
116. Revelation 7:15 NIV.
117. James Moffatt, *A New Translation of the Bible Containing the Old and New Testaments* (New York: Harper & Row Publishers, 1954), 315.
118. Harry Ironside, *Overshadowed*, copyright 1935 by Geo. S. Schuler in *Pastor Ironside's Gospel Songs*. Assigned to Singspiration, Inc.
119. Revelation 7:17.
120. Phillip W. Keller, *A Shepherd Looks at Psalm 23* (Minneapolis: World Wide Publications, 1970), 21–22.
121. Peterson, *Reversed Thunder*, 85–86.
122. Revelation 8:1.
123. Revelation 8:2.
124. Revelation 8:3–4.
125. Exodus 30:34.
126. Revelation 8:5–9:21.
127. Peterson, *Reversed Thunder*, 88.
128. Psalm 74:10.
129. Revelation 6:10b.
130. "Full Story of Youcef Nadarkhani," *International Christian Concern*, November 1, 2010, http://www.persecution.org/2010/11/02/full-story-of-youcef-nadarkhani/.
131. Michael Ireland, "Iran Claims Pastor Nadarkhani Won't Be Executed," *ASSIST News Service*, http://www.assistnews.net/Stories/2012/s12030077.htm.
132. Ephesians 3:8.
133. Revelation 5:2.
134. Revelation 10:1–4.
135. 1 Corinthians 13:12 NLT.
136. Peterson, *Reversed Thunder*, 106–107.
137. Matthew 10:16.
138. Colossians 4:6.
139. Ephesians 5:16.
140. Revelation 10:5–11.
141. Ezekiel 3:1–4, 7–12a, 14a *The Message*.
142. Revelation 11:1–10 NIV.
143. Revelation 11:10.
144. Matthew 5:11, 12.
145. Revelation 11:11–14.
146. Revelation 11:13b.

147. Revelation 9:20–21.
148. See Psalm 18:28–29.
149. Revelation 11:15–19 NIV.
150. See, for example, Luke 21:25–28.
151. Luke 21:29–32.
152. Revelation 12:1–2.
153. Revelation 12:3–4a.
154. Revelation 12:4b–6.
155. Revelation 12:7–12.
156. Revelation 13:1–2.
157. 2 Corinthians 10:3–5.
158. Matthew 21:21.
159. James 5:16 KJV.
160. James 2:13.
161. 1 Corinthians 13:13.
162. Matthew 4:1–11.
163. Revelation 13:10b.
164. Revelation 13:11.
165. Revelation 13:12–17 NIV.
166. Revelation 13:18.
167. Peterson, *Reversed Thunder*, 126.
168. Revelation 14:1–5.
169. Revelation 14:6–10a.
170. Revelation 14:12.
171. Revelation 14:14–20.
172. 2 Peter 3:9 *The Message*.
173. 1 Thessalonians 5:2.
174. Revelation 15:1–8.
175. Revelation 16:1.
176. Exodus 9:13.
177. Revelation 16:9.
178. Revelation 16:10b–11 NIV.
179. Revelation 16:21b.
180. 2 Thessalonians 1:6–7 *The Message*.
181. Revelation 16:5–6.
182. Revelation 16:7.
183. Revelation 17:3–6a.
184. Revelation 17:15.
185. Revelation 18:21–24.
186. Revelation 19:2 KJV.
187. Revelation 19:1–6.
188. Revelation 19:7–10.
189. John 3:28–29 NLT.
190. Matthew 9:14–15 NLT.
191. 2 Corinthians 11:2 EVS.
192. Revelation 19:11–21.

193. C. S. Lewis, *The Lion, the Witch and the Wardrobe* (New York: HarperCollins 1994), 181–183.
194. Peterson, *Reversed Thunder*, 161.
195. Thomas Kelly, "Happy Those Who Trust in Jesus," public domain.
196. Sabine Baring-Gould, "Onward, Christian Soldiers," public domain.
197. Peterson, *Reversed Thunder*, 166.
198. Branko Milanovic, *The Haves and the Have-Nots* (New York: Basic Books, 2011), 168–169.
199. Revelation 21:1 NIV.
200. Revelation 21:2–5 NIV.
201. Ezekiel 37:27 EVS.
202. Revelation 21:6–8 NIV.
203. Revelation 21:9–14.
204. Daniel 12:3 *The Message*.
205. Ezekiel 40:2 EVS.
206. Revelation 21:15–27 NIV.
207. Earl F. Palmer, *The Communicator's Commentary: Revelation* (Waco: Word Books, 1982), 251.
208. Revelation 22:1–5.
209. 1 Corinthians 13:12.
210. Revelation 22:5a NCV.
211. Tim Lahaye, *Revelation Explained* (Grand Rapids: Zondervan, 1999), 369.
212. 2 Corinthians 4:17.
213. Revelation 22:6–21.
214. Revelation 1:1–3.
215. Revelation 22:7b.
216. Ibid.
217. Revelation 22:8–9.
218. Peterson, *Reversed Thunder*, 186.
219. Revelation 22:7b.
220. Rory Noland, *Worship on Earth as It Is in Heaven* (Grand Rapids: Zondervan, 2011), 218.
221. Revelation 22:7, 12, 20.
222. Matthew 26:64.
223. Mark 13:33a KJV.
224. John 14:3a KJV.
225. Revelation 1:7a.
226. Revelation 3:11a.
227. Revelation 16:15a.
228. Earl F. Palmer, *The Communicator's Commentary: Revelation* (Waco: Word Books, 1982), 251.
229. Revelation 22:17a.
230. Revelation 22:17b.
231. Revelation 22:17b *The Message*.
232. Isaiah 12:3 *The Message*.
233. Luke 10:1.